WHAT'S YOUR CREATIVE TYPE?

WHAT'S YOUR CREATIVE TYPE?

Harness the Power of Your
Artistic Personality

by
META WAGNER

SEAL PRESS

ISBN: 978-1-58005-637-3 (paperback)
ISBN: 978-1-58005-638-0 (e-book)
Library of Congress Cataloging-in-Publication Data for this book is
available.

Published by SEAL PRESS, an imprint of Perseus Books, LLC,
a subsidiary of Hachette Book Group, Inc.
1700 Fourth Street, Berkeley, California 94710
sealpress.com

Cover Design: Kara Davison
Interior Design: Jack Lenzo

Printed in the United States of America
Distributed by Hachette Book Group

10 9 8 7 6 5 4 3 2 1

For my mother (long gone but always with me) and father:
the greatest cheerleaders for creativity I could have ever asked for.

CONTENTS

INTRODUCTION

To create a work of art is to create the world.

—WASSILY KANDINSKY, *CONCERNING THE SPIRITUAL IN ART*

Do any of these descriptions fit you?

You're the funniest person no one knows. Well, your friends know you, and they think you're hilarious. They keep saying you could be the next Louis C.K. or Amy Schumer—with a Seinfeldian twist. You figure your dream of becoming a stand-up comic (with your own sketch comedy show someday) is childish and impractical. Yet, if you developed five minutes of material, you just might bring down the house at Chuckles Comedy Club, and who knows where that could lead.

Or, you've got a dirty little secret: for months you were drafting a novel, even getting up at five most mornings to write before leaving for your office job. But, you couldn't decide if your thriller was brilliant or worthless, and so you stopped writing, mid-sentence, on page 84 (the sentence reads, "And then she picked up the knife he'd just sharpened yesterday and plunged it into _____"). Yet every now and then when you come across the folder in your documents named "First Novel," your pulse races and you swear you can feel the adrenalin course through your veins and you move the cursor so it hovers over that damn folder . . . but something keeps you from clicking on it.

Or, you've made it! You've had a successful career as a painter—
one of your paintings even hangs in the Contemporary Arts Center in Cincinnati—and you've had some gallery shows over the
years in Boston and Philly and once in Tokyo. One well-known art
critic even called you a twenty-first-century Salvador Dali. It's not
how you see yourself, but you saved the link and held on to the clip-
ping anyway. You've even managed to make a solid living doing the
thing you love. Lately, however, you worry you're losing your mojo
and a new generation of artists is getting all the commissions—and
threatening to put you *out* of commission.

If these or similar tales of woe feel familiar to you, congratu-
lations! You're following in the grand tradition of creative masters
throughout the centuries who also struggled to get going, overcome doubts, or stay motivated over the long run. Did you know,
for instance, that, before he penned *Leaves of Grass* at the mid-
point of his life, Walt Whitman was a jack-of-all-trades: carpenter,
schoolteacher, printer, journalist, and the author of a "temperance"
novel? One critic even commented, "Whitman was a non-poet in
every way, with no mark of special talent or temperament." Or that
Georgia O'Keeffe was hospitalized for extreme anxiety over the
mural she was commissioned to paint for Radio City Music Hall?
Or that Frank Sinatra prematurely retired, twenty-two years before the true end of his career, even leaving the stage with the lyrics
from the song "Angel Eyes," "Excuse me while I disappear"? And
yet, they all entered the pantheon of creative gods.

What allowed these artists to pursue their passion despite
their doubts and fears?

Each of them possessed something beyond pure talent, dedication, opportunity, or luck, something you may not have identified
within yourself … *yet*: These creators knew *why* they created.

They were conscious of their motives, their purpose, their
goals. Many even spoke and wrote with impressive insight about

their *why*. An understanding of their motivations was the driving force behind their work, and it's what propelled each of them to such wondrous heights. This awareness—and the subsequent creative boosts—is a trait that defines countless prolific, powerful, satisfied artists.

So, if you want to enhance *your* creativity and reach *your* artistic potential, you, too, must first understand why you create.

Whether you're a student with artistic inclinations, an accomplished artist who's weighing the next steps in your career, a Gen Xer or Boomer who wonders why you ever gave up playing the sax or drawing pastel landscapes (activities you once *loved*), or a retiree tentatively trying quilting or jazz dance for the first time, understanding your artistic motivations matters. And recognizing your fears and self-defeating tendencies matters, too.

Think of it this way: In most areas of your life you're probably pretty clear about why you do the things you do, right? When it comes to being creative, however, most people haven't thought about why it's important to them—they just know it is. Yet, doing something in the arts isn't a requirement. No one's demanding you become a poet or painter or videogame designer. Also, as you've probably noticed, creativity is not the most surefire way of earning an income. Regardless, history shows us people will find a way, somehow, to pursue their artistic passions against all odds. There must be reasons for this sort of dogged devotion.

Your own desire to express yourself creatively is a case in point. You could be sitting on the couch night after night, binge-watching all eighteen seasons so far of *Law & Order: SVU*. (Not that there's anything wrong with that!) Instead, something calls to you, gets under your skin, makes you reach for your journal and scribble notes for your novel, audition for the role of Mimi in your school's production of *Rent*, knit a scarf of your own intricate design, or write lyrics with a powerful feminist message.

When you're able to scratch your artistic itch, nothing's better. But when the words aren't flowing or you feel like no one "gets" you or the tickets aren't selling, it's frustrating and ego-deflating. In those moments, it's hard not to feel discouraged, even despondent, and these feelings can make it hard for you to move forward on a project. Writers, at least, have a term for when they're feeling stuck: "writer's block." But creative people of all stripes experience that same awful feeling of stuckness at times.

And, so, knowing why you create—figuring out your impulses and drives and motivations—and also becoming aware of your creativity-killing fears and attitudes can make all the difference between giving up and doing the imaginative work you really want to do. It can lead you to the relief and satisfaction that comes when you've made it through an impasse—that *ahhhhhhh* feeling—that makes the struggle worthwhile.

The Concept of Creative Types

And now we've come to the heart of the matter: identifying your creative type. A creative type is an artistic personality profile based on what motivates a person to do creative work. The concept of motivation types grew out of the extensive research and thinking I've done for a seminar I teach at Emerson College, "Creativity in Context," which explores the question, "Why do people create?" It struck me that most studies of creativity focus on *how* artists create, not *why*. And yet, the why is so important! And so I embarked on a search for what artists and writers themselves have said about their personal motivations and developed my curriculum, which reflected their perspectives and insights.

After seeing how my students over the years have responded to the course (enthusiastically, I'm happy to report!), I realized I'd tapped into something valuable for anyone with creative leanings. In analyzing past and present artistic greats, I identified their most common drives and realized they could be grouped under five distinct artistic personality types. And thus the idea of creative types—and this book—was born.

I hope reading about creative types—and identifying your own—will make your path to artistic self-discovery entertaining as well as illuminating. If you've spent any time on social media surveys attempting to determine your literary twin, Harry Potter house, or U.S. president alter ego, you already know what fun it is to use typology. Here, using typology, backed by theories and examples, will also bring you real, lifelong benefits.

So, here's a sneak peek at the creative types!

The Five Creative Types

Which one do you think you might be?

- The A-Lister
- The Artisan
- The Game Changer
- The Sensitive Soul
- The Activist

The A-Lister. A-Listers seek ego fulfillment—and why not? The ego is a powerful, undeniable force. A-Listers relish being the center of attention. They want to have an emotional impact on their audience and, in return, receive the applause and love and adoration of their fans. That is what sustains them. They entertain fantasies of fame and wealth and may even achieve them. If they can't live forever, they hope their name and their novels, paintings, songs, or films will.

The Artisan. Artisans believe being creative is its own reward. The process brings them joy, even bliss. They get so immersed in their art that they lose all sense of time or place. There's no higher high for them than finding the right rhyme, brush stroke, or tap technique. They treasure predecessors who've influenced them, and they're open to collaboration with current artists. They love what they do, and they treat it as serious work, not just play. They feel lucky they get to do the thing they love.

The Game Changer. Game Changers strive to produce something new and startling in art. They possess both the ego drive of the A-Lister and the devotion of the Artisan. Nothing pleases them more than breaking boundaries and crashing conventions. They're pioneers and will hold firm to their vision whether anyone else understands it or not… critics and audiences will surely come around. While Game Changers are individualists, they also make for great leaders of movements and writers of manifestos that declare war on art's past and lay out the possibilities for a more expansive future.

The Sensitive Soul. Sensitive Souls brim with emotion, and they pour it into creative outlets. Their sensitivity and depth of feeling are essential to their artistic pursuits. Sensitive Souls use art to explore their own life histories and experiences and to make meaning of them and possibly achieve some catharsis. Creativity may even help them escape from too much solitude at times. Their art has the potential to change people's lives and inspire, comfort, or help heal them.

The Activist. Activists use their creativity to change the world. They are fired up and ready to go. Everywhere they look, they see wrongs that need righting, and they'll use their art to try to do just that: eliminate poverty, advance civil rights, or end wars. They aren't content with making silly love songs or pretty pictures, not when the world is such a mess. Activists are willing to risk their reputations, or even their very freedom, to produce art with political purpose.

Maybe, as you read about these creative types, one jumped out at you and you thought, "Yes, that's me!" Or, you saw traits of each within yourself, with one type predominating. Perhaps one type best describes the younger you but, as you matured, you acquired the characteristics of a different type. All of these ways of thinking about your artistic personality are legit.

What to Expect

In the following pages, you'll learn about the five creative types in greater depth, with each chapter devoted to one particular type. Warning: no artistic personality is free from some good-natured ribbing!

You'll receive answers to questions, explore issues, and learn how to prepare for any setbacks you might face. Creative theorists and psychologists will weigh in. You'll read stories about famous creators across the arts spectrum, including Pablo Picasso, Sylvia Plath, Francis Ford Coppola, Beyoncé, and Lin-Manuel Miranda, along with many, many others. These creators share a lot of your traits and tendencies, so their stories will teach you what to do—and, just as importantly, what not to do—in keeping with your artistic personality. You'll gain insights and advice from them, taken from interviews, essays, journal entries, and letters. And, every now and then I'll jump in with stories from my career as a teacher and columnist.

You'll see creativity boosters—ideas and exercises to jump-start your creativity—and suggestions for how to nurture your positive tendencies and tame your self-defeating ones. And you'll get to take personality-style quizzes to help you discover your artistic motivations and answer the all-important question: What's your creative type? So, get started! Go to the chapter on the creative type that speaks most forcefully to you, and then read the rest of the chapters to learn about additional aspects of yourself and others in your artistic community, including potential collaborators and competitors. Or, read straight through (or from back to front if you're a rebellious Game Changer!). You'll notice the Conclusion contains valuable insights and stories that apply across the board, to all creative types.

However you approach this book, I hope you'll have fun, learn a lot, and, most of all, discover your artistic personality so you can embrace a life filled with creativity.

Chapter 1

THE A-LISTER: SEEKING APPLAUSE & ADORATION, FAME & IMMORTALITY

ᴡᴧᵔ

The only people who are remembered
are kings, criminals, and artists.

—Eric Bogosian, *The Perforated Heart*

Do you ever fantasize about doing a reading of your debut novel before packed venues across the country? The very novel *New York Times* book critic Michiko Kakutani hailed as both "deeply felt" and "a rollicking delight"? Perhaps you're hoping your studio arts professor at Parsons School of Design, the one who told you you're "marginally talented," will see your painting, *One Apple, One Desire*, on the cover of *ARTnews*. Better yet, he'll post a Facebook comment saying he knew all along you had "it." Or, you believe you could be the next Meryl Streep (or Beyoncé, or Martin Scorsese, or J. D. Salinger) of your generation.

You just might be an A-Lister.

Why Do A-Listers Create?

If you're an A-Lister or you have those tendencies, you feel driven to write, dance, direct, film, compose, or do other forms of art for so many reasons, most of which come down to your ego. And that's okay! After all, where would any of us be without a strong, healthy (some might say overweening) ego? See if these reasons for creating strike a chord with you.

You create because the adoration of your parents, partner, or children is not nearly enough to satisfy you. Because your ballet teacher insisted you were too heavy/short/curvy to ever make it as a prima ballerina. Because you saw Springsteen rock out for three-plus hours, and, damn, you knew you had to be onstage. Because you want others to see what you see, feel what you feel, or think what you think. ("Who wouldn't?" is probably what you're thinking right now.) Because your mother laughed at a joke you made when you were four and you want to recapture that feeling over and over and over again. Because you want to feel alive. Because you want to be remembered after you die. Because you believe you've been given a gift, and it's your duty to share it with the world. Because you might even want to play God.

Snapshot of an A-Lister

An A-Lister's ego is not to be trifled with. It's shouting, I'm here, I matter. What I think, believe, observe, interpret, draw, write, sing matters because I matter.

You're an A-Lister if you have the "audacity" to believe you have something of value to share, something dazzling, bold, emotive, or enlightening. Something you—and only you—can convey.

A-Listers need to share their art with the world because, after all, if a tree falls in the woods and no one hears it, what's the point of being a tree? Let others keep a drawer full of unpublished scripts or perform as Stella in a community theater production of *A Streetcar Named Desire*, but not the A-Listers. They're Broadway-bound! The A-Lister knows that an artist without a big ego is like a Maserati without a twin turbo engine. How would it run? How would *you* run?

They also know there's no reason to apologize for their grand vision, their unstoppable ambition, their "I'll show *them*" mantra.

No two A-Listers are identical. Some are overbearing, others are divinely charismatic. Some are needy for people's approval, others want to give the audience all they've got. Some are prolific, others have had one grand masterpiece and are then paralyzed with fear of failure. But they all tend to place more stock in the finished product than the process because the product is the glory.

However, if you're an A-Lister whose ego is too tightly tied to your artistic output, you could be in for a rough ride. Your productivity could slow or temporarily disappear, or audiences might no longer clamor for you—and then what? A huge ego can easily be deflated. You might also be driven by dark feelings like the desire to enact revenge or trounce a competitor, and these distracting motives could derail your creative aims.

But, all in all, you've got a lot going for you, A-Lister. The ego is a powerful force, and it can propel you to great heights.

Varieties of A-Listers

You might be the sort of A-Lister who keeps quiet about your aspirations (even your best friend would be surprised to hear you

Artistic Personality Quiz
So, You Think You're an A-Lister

1. Do you fantasize about any of the following: the spotlight on you and you alone, a standing ovation and shouts of "bravo" or "brava," amazing reviews, fangirls or -boys, millions of social media followers, your own reality TV show, and/or boatloads of money?
2. Are you most alive when you're creating or performing for people?
3. Do you want to be a star, not "just" an actor/painter/writer?
4. Are you hoping to prove someone wrong who told you one of the following: "You're not all that talented," "You'll never make it as an artist," or "You can't make money from art"?
5. Do you long to create a work of art or give a performance that will make people laugh uncontrollably, sob, or feel forever changed?
6. Do you hope people will be talking about you and your art decades, or even centuries, from now?
7. Do you believe a gift of talent has been bestowed on you from on high?
8. Does competition stoke your creative fire?
9. Do you treasure the finished product even more than the creative process?
10. Do you enjoy "playing God" by giving life to and controlling your artistic work and/or the lives of your fictional characters?
11. Is remaining relevant to the culture at large important to you?

If you answered "yes" to most of these questions, you are an A-Lister. And if you answered "yes" to even a few of these questions, you have some strong A-Lister tendencies. Either way, read on.

consider yourself this type). Or, you might be the kind of A-Lister who chews up the scenery or sucks all the oxygen out of the room. Maybe, for you, there's nothing like a live audience—you feed off their energy and adore the sight of their faces beaming up at you. Or, maybe you enjoy manipulating people into feeling certain feelings or believing what you want them to believe. These are some of the traits that differentiate one A-Lister from another.

See the Sidebar for a list of varieties of A-Listers, and read on for an exploration of some of the most common ones.

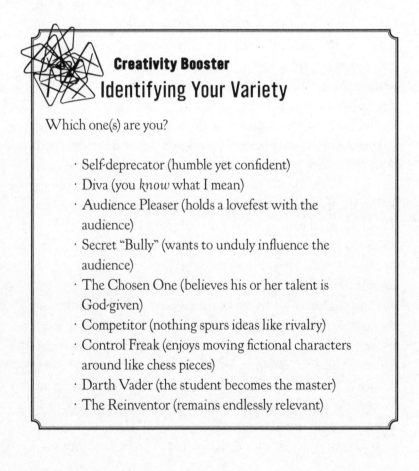

Creativity Booster
Identifying Your Variety

Which one(s) are you?

- Self-deprecator (humble yet confident)
- Diva (you *know* what I mean)
- Audience Pleaser (holds a lovefest with the audience)
- Secret "Bully" (wants to unduly influence the audience)
- The Chosen One (believes his or her talent is God-given)
- Competitor (nothing spurs ideas like rivalry)
- Control Freak (enjoys moving fictional characters around like chess pieces)
- Darth Vader (the student becomes the master)
- The Reinventor (remains endlessly relevant)

The A-Lister Spectrum: Where Do You Belong?

Picture a horizontal line with people placed at different points along the egoism spectrum. All the way to the left is the humble-seeming A-Lister, and all the way to the right is what some might call the braggart.

The singer Adele might assume a place at far left because, while she's got a magnetic stage presence and feeds off the love and adulation of her audience, she's willing to turn down high-visibility opportunities like the 2017 Super Bowl (as she put it, the half-time show's not really about music). She's also the queen of self-deprecating humor and suffers from terrible stage fright. Those are qualities that keep an ego in check. And while she relishes the attention, she can live for long periods without it—which certainly cannot be said of all A-Listers.

In 2011, Adele's doctor ordered her to stop singing, or even talking, for weeks after surgery to remove a polyp on her vocal cord. And then, once her son was born the following year, she chose to live a low-profile life for a while so she could take care of him. While the stage and recording studio beckoned to her, she resisted its call. As for the diva behavior that defines a lot of A-Listers? You just never hear about Adele trashing hotel rooms or pitching a fit if bottles of Cristal aren't placed in ice buckets backstage during her concert tours!

You might pick an artist like the rapper Kanye West to occupy the position on the far right of the spectrum. He's an obvious choice and one my students often make when I ask them to name an ego-driven artist. In addition to West's notorious attention-grabbing behavior, he's also directly compared himself to Steve Jobs, Anna Wintour, and Michelangelo, among other overachievers. And, he named his sixth studio album, *Yeezus* (which I'll leave you to interpret). So, it's pretty safe to say Kanye has A-Lister tendencies of a pronounced nature. It's also safe to say these very same tendencies have helped make him one of the most successful and admired musicians of a generation. What's the level of attention you need? Where would you place yourself on the A-Lister spectrum?

The Audience Pleaser

As an A-Lister, the form of creativity you're most drawn to—and the degree of audience responsiveness it invites—might be a clue to your deepest needs. Understanding this about yourself is not only interesting; it can help guide you toward the forms of creative expression and careers that suit you best.

Here's what I mean. There are three types of artistic expression: (1) with an immediate audience reaction (live performance), (2) with an audience but with delayed feedback (writing, painting, acting in movies), and (3) without an audience (the proverbial novel that sits in a drawer—definitely not for A-Listers).

Which of the first two choices indicates a greater need for ego fulfillment? Take the example of an actor or actress. You could say a movie actor has a larger ego than a stage actor because he or she is more likely to have "movie star looks" and to be in pursuit of stardom, a lavish lifestyle, fifty million Twitter followers, and so on.

And, yet, isn't it the stage performer who feeds off a live audience's responses—laughter, muffled crying, applause, standing ovations, and whistles of approval—who is actually more ego-driven?

Consider actress Susan Sarandon's unabashed explanation of the difference between acting in a film or in theater, as revealed in an interview with The Telegraph: "It's like the difference between masturbation and making love. When you're in movies you are almost by yourself, whereas on stage you have a relationship with the audience." I bet you never thought of the difference that way before, right? But, you probably see the truth in Sarandon's statement because it conveys the desire for instant connection many performers crave, one that feeds their ego.

In a *New York* magazine interview, actress Glenn Close described the relationship between a performer and her audience as follows: "Good live theater disturbs molecules. You create an energy source around yourself and it alternates between you and the audience. Anybody who sees live theater should come out a little rearranged."

Patti LuPone clearly craves such a connection with a live audience. While she has played various roles on television, her first love is the Broadway stage, where her powerhouse performances have wowed audiences for years. She thrives on the intensity of acting and singing before a live audience (except, as she's made clear, when they're talking, texting, or taking photos on their phones during a performance, as was made obvious in a viral video of LuPone grabbing an audience member's phone).

During an interview with LuPone, NPR correspondent Susan Stamberg told the actress a story about a friend who brought her daughter to see LuPone in the musical *Gypsy* on Broadway. Naturally, as is typical of tweens, the daughter was acting as if she wanted nothing to do with her mom. But, when LuPone started singing "Rose's Turn," the daughter grabbed her mother's wrist. They were both, in the mom's words, transported. When LuPone heard the story, she cried. She knew her performance had left the girl feeling more than a little "rearranged."

In the documentary *Elaine Stritch: Shoot Me*, the Broadway icon said the best part about performing was receiving the audience's love. And comedian Dave Chappelle, whose honesty and poignancy on an episode of *Inside the Actors Studio* has made it a fan favorite, conveyed how his audience keeps him going. He got a little emotional as he described it, saying, "You're standing up there . . .

like a gladiator, and them lights is on you, and you look down, and everyone's looking up at you like 'Ahhhhh.' ... They love you, man, you know? It's like a—it's a lovefest. Yeah, it's the best feeling. I love stand-up."

If you're an audience-pleasing A-Lister, there's no denying that you crave a good lovefest. You just need to figure out which kind is most satisfying for you.

The "Secret Bully"

Not every A-Lister, however, needs or even wants the connection with his or her audience to be so blatant. For them there's another approach, as you'll see.

Several decades of writer Joan Didion's journalism, personal essays, novels, screenplays, and, later, memoirs have made her not only a writer's writer but also a literary icon for legions of fans. (Read "Goodbye to All That" from her collection *Slouching Towards Bethlehem*, and you'll understand why.)

If you've seen Didion in person or in photographs, you were no doubt struck by how thin she is—fragile, even. But her fragility belies a hidden strength. You'll see what I mean when you read what she has to say about the ego drive in her 1976 piece for *The New York Times Magazine*, "Why I Write," a title taken from George Orwell's timeless essay.

Didion writes, "In many ways writing is the act of saying *I*, of imposing oneself upon other people, of saying *listen to me, see it my way, change your mind*. It's an aggressive, even hostile act." She continues, "You can disguise its aggressiveness all you want ... with the whole manner of intimating rather than claiming, of alluding rather than stating—but there's no getting around the fact that setting words on paper is the tactic of a secret bully, an invasion, an imposition of the writer's sensibility on the reader's most private space."

Writers are bullies? Writers, who hide behind their computer screens and keep their noses buried in books and sometimes use pen names to camouflage their identities and only give up their favorite window seat at Starbucks to stumble out into the world at closing time, over-caffeinated and pale... they're *bullies?*

Obviously not schoolyard bullies who trip and push and beat up their targets. Not mean girl bullies who gossip and insinuate and ignore. Not cyberbullies who seek to hurt and humiliate. *Secret* bullies. *Clever* bullies. One might even say *passive-aggressive* bullies who impose their sensibility on an unsuspecting reader without the reader even realizing he or she has been "attacked." Didion's not only speaking of opinion writers and cultural commentators who are obvious in their appeal to readers to *listen to me, see it my way, change your mind.* She's referring to *all* writers and, I'd venture to say, all artists.

In an interview in the *Paris Review,* Didion further explained her perspective, saying, "It's hostile to try to wrench around someone else's mind that way." She compared this situation to one in which someone is trying to describe his or her dream to another person who simply isn't interested in it, and observed, "The writer is always tricking the reader into listening to the dream."

Think about a time when you came to the last lines of a novel, let's say Jane Austen's *Pride and Prejudice,* and you were bereft because you could no longer live in the British Regency world of the Bennet family. Jane Austen secretly bullied you. And if you've watched TV shows like *The Sopranos* or *House of Cards* and found yourself time and again rooting for the bad guy, even as he blithely murdered his way through the series, the shows' creators bullied you.

For an A-Lister, bullying means inducing (some might say "manipulating") a response, especially an emotional one, in the audience. In the play *Red,* the lead character, based on the real-life painter

Creativity Booster
Becoming a Secret Bully

What's a creative project you're working on now or hope to do in the future? How does it allow you to be a secret bully? If you're making a short documentary about your grandmother's struggle with Parkinson's disease and plan to post it on You-Tube, for example, you hope viewers will learn valuable information or be moved to tears. During your stand-up act, you want audience members to laugh so hard they double over in pain (though that might be venturing into *actual* bully territory). The protagonist of your television script does awful, shameful things, but you want the audience to love him anyway. Any of these scenarios and many others could be your induction into secret bullyhood. Here's your opportunity to do in art what is so difficult to do in real life: get away with bullying people!

But here's some advice to make sure you don't become overbearing: If you write an opinion piece, you could present a counterargument to convey your reasonableness (followed by a rousing rebuttal, of course). If you develop characters who are sure to win your readers' hearts, try to avoid crossing over into tearjerker territory. Whatever genre of art you're doing, remember: it's a fine line between subtle artistic persuasion and outright harassment of your audience.

Mark Rothko, bellows at his assistant, Ken: "I am here to stop your heart, you understand that? I am here to make you think.... I am not here to make pretty pictures!" This sums up some A-Listers' desire to bully their audience into the desired reaction quite well, I'd say.

The Chosen People

How often have you heard winners at the Grammy or Tony Awards thank God for the talent bestowed upon them? Are you hoping that will be you someday? While it might appear humble to share credit with a higher power, it also means you believe you were personally selected by that higher power for special powers of your own. Very A-Listy!

Queen of Soul Aretha Franklin once said, "Being a singer is a natural gift. It means I'm using to the highest degree possible the gift that God gave me to use. I'm happy with that." Photographer Robert Mapplethorpe, in describing his process, made the spiritual connection more personal, saying, "When I work, and in my art, I hold hands with God" and "I stand naked when I draw. God holds my hand and we sing together." These statements must have infuri-ated the people who found his breakthrough homoerotic portraits in the 1970s particularly ungodlike.

And here's my favorite example, again featuring Patti LuPone. She wondered aloud to a reporter at *Time Out* why casting direc-tors don't always think of her for a role she's clearly suited for, say-ing, "I *know* how good I am, and that's not a boast. This is a gift from God that I've had since I was four years old." Well, it might be a boast, but, then again, it's justified.

You, too, may believe you've received a gift from God, whether it's your perfect pitch or your gravity-defying grand jetés. But, more important than where your talent came from is where you'll go with it—and where it might take you.

Positive Tendencies of A-Listers

Celebrating the Ego

In writer Bertrand Russell's acceptance speech for the 1950 Nobel Prize in Literature, he addressed what he considered the four key human desires: acquisitiveness, rivalry, vanity, and love of power. As you might have suspected, these match closely with an A-Lister's drives. I like what he had to say about vanity, in particular: "Vanity is a motive of immense potency. Anyone who has much to do with children knows how they are constantly performing some antic, and saying 'Look at me.' 'Look at me' is one of the most fundamental desires of the human heart. It can take innumerable forms, from buffoonery to the pursuit of posthumous fame."

I'm going to hope and assume that you, dear A-Lister, are no buffoon, but I'll bet you have a lot of "look at me" in you, no matter your age. Good for you! You're meant to occupy center stage and you know it.

Is it any wonder, then, that in his essay "Why I Write," George Orwell lists "sheer egoism" as the first of his four motives for writing? (The others are "aesthetic enthusiasm," "historical impulse," and "political purpose.") I believe Orwell was speaking for other writers, too, and, by extension, artists in any field. He defines "sheer egoism" as the "desire to seem clever, to be talked about, to be remembered after death, to get your own back on the grown-ups who snubbed you in childhood, etc., etc."

This philosophy sounds current, but it took root in the experiences of young Eric Arthur Blair in the early 1900s, years before he assumed the nom de plume George Orwell. Feeling overlooked and isolated might have been the undoing of another child. But, in Orwell's case, it was painful yet productive. Who can say if he'd have written the classic novels *Animal Farm* and *1984* if he'd felt appreciated as a child?

Orwell also believed that most people beyond the age of thirty give up their individualism and their dreams and live primarily for others. Writers, however, belong to a class of people who defy this stereotype.

A-Lister, if you forgive Orwell his elitism, you'll appreciate his takedown of the majority of over-thirties around the world who apparently live lives of quiet desperation. You can take refuge in the knowledge that he doesn't mean *you*, no matter your age. Better yet, you'll see he is a true admirer of the A-Lister's sense of self, even if others might perceive it as "selfish."

Is being ego-driven selfish? I like to think of it more as self-directed. (Doesn't that sound better?) Besides, the harsh reality of the arts is that, unless you're already famous, no one's sitting around waiting for the moment when you'll write your novel, produce your film, or choreograph your dance. The world would still spin on its axis whether you pursued your passion or not. It's all on you. In fact, you *need* some swagger to believe that you have something unique to offer; you'll fill stadiums, theaters, or galleries someday; the characters drawn from your imagination will leave an enduring mark on literature; and you'll become a household name. When you consider that you're in a competition of sorts with all the amazing art and music that is centuries old and still popular today, plus all the current artists trying to make a name for themselves, your A-Lister's ego gives you a distinct advantage. Call it selfish or self-directed, egoism is the A-Lister's strong suit, so get your swagger on.

Taking a Selfie

Turning your life into a work of art—memoir, personal essay, "thinly disguised" fiction, self-portrait, stand-up routine, even reality TV show—can help you or your audience come to insightful realizations, learn to cope, or feel less alone (see Chapter 4, "The Sensitive Soul," if the alleviation of loneliness speaks to you). But for you it's also a way to celebrate, well, you!

As an A-Lister, you've probably done a lot of living, and you've got entertaining stories to keep your friends endlessly amused. You might have a sense of yourself not only as a person but also a persona, a personality. You were the kid in class pictures who was always mugging for the camera. You were the one practicing a monologue about your crazy family in front of a full-length mirror, with your hairbrush-microphone in hand. And, you're the one who believes there are few occasions when a selfie isn't called for.

This A-Lister tendency to celebrate the self isn't new. Centuries before Kim Kardashian perfected the art of the selfie, the Dutch painter Rembrandt van Rijn was doing the same, and for a similar mix of reasons: self-discovery, artistry, and, yes, publicity. Over the course of four decades, he made an astounding number of self-portraits (approximately eighty) in various media, including paintings, drawings, and prints. There was the "artist as a young man," full of vitality; the middle-aged man wearing the clothes and accessories that fame bought him, such as gold chains, embroidered shirts, and fur-trimmed velvet coats; and, finally, the older, more introspective Rembrandt.

Art historian James Hall, in his book, *The Self-Portrait: A Cultural History*, has identified a strong self-promotional strategy behind these scores of selfies. He says of Rembrandt, "His early self-portrait prints are sent all over the place, so everyone would have known what he looked like even if they'd never seen another work by Rembrandt. As an independent artist, not a court artist, he had to make more of an effort to put himself on the map. Making a self-portrait suggests that you are already famous even if you're not."

Nurture Your Tendencies
Take a Selfie That Matters

An A-Lister who isn't center stage is a sad A-Lister indeed. So, make sure the spotlight is on you, but, like Rembrandt, back up your bid for attention with real substance. If you think your life lends itself to a great memoir or play, strive to create work that goes beyond me-me-me and strikes some universal chords. If you're someone who has been told, "You're a real character," make your quirkiness the basis for your art (think of Woody Allen's success at doing this). Remember, A-Lister, you have an unbreakable pact with your audience: you've got to create something meaningful to them, and they'll give you their adoration in return.

Achieving Immortality Through Art

How amazing would it be to defy death, if not in body, then in your paintings or songs or poems—art that will leave an impression on generations of people to come?

Art can, like children, be your mark on the world, proving you were here and the world is forever changed because you lived in it. You birthed beings, or art, no one else has or ever will.

This thought may not occupy the minds of all artistic people. Most are trying to be creative and get their work noticed and make a few bucks from it. The idea of producing art that will be read, viewed, or listened to centuries or even millennia later is not at the forefront of their minds.

And then there are the A-Listers.

Art challenges death, flies in the face of death, makes a mockery of death—even though some of its most famous practitioners succumbed too early to death. Not content to merely make it in this lifetime, A-Listers want to keep making it even once they've "shuffled off this mortal coil" (fittingly, a phrase from *Hamlet* by the mortality-defying playwright William Shakespeare). Many A-Listers are well aware of their desire to live on through their works. Singer Bob Marley claimed, "My music will go on forever." Author Jorge Luis Borges said, "When writers die they become books, which is, after all, not too bad an incarnation." Writer James Salter said, "Life passes into pages if it passes into anything." And poet and novelist Sylvia Plath captured similar sentiments in her journal, noting, "Writing is a religious act: it is an ordering, a reforming, a relearning and reloving of people and the world as they are and as they might be. A shaping which does not pass away like a day of typing or a day of teaching. The writing lasts: it goes about on its own in the world. People read it: react to it as to a person, a philosophy, a religion, a flower."

Keep in mind that the desire for immortality is not only about attaining everlasting fame, however. As an A-Lister, it's also about your strong ego attachment to your work and belief in it and, if you're a novelist, screenwriter, or playwright, a true bond with your characters. Isn't it strange to think that people have a limited life span while the characters imagined by a writer might live forever? And, yet, it's so.

Immortality through your art is not beyond your reach, especially today when much of what you produce will be recorded. Just think: someone in the twenty-second century might appreciate your work every bit as much as a twenty-first-century audience member. It doesn't get much better than that, A-Lister!

Competitive, Much?

A-Listers take to competition the way a lapsed vegan takes to a hunk of sirloin—that is to say, with great gusto. They vie for superiority, even with their former, younger, more energetic, and prolific selves. And, naturally, their competitive spirit really comes to the fore in jockeying with their artistic predecessors or their contemporaries. The competition might be friendly or vicious. Sometimes the rivalry is purely in the mind of one artist, but at other times it's an all-out battle of the bards… or songwriters.

A renowned friendly competition in which both artists benefited was the one between John Lennon and Paul McCartney, specifically as songwriters. In the book *A Day in the Life* by Mark Hertsgaard, the Beatles' producer George Martin described their partnership this way: "Imagine two people pulling on a rope … smiling at each other and pulling all the time with all their might. The tension between the two of them made for the bond."

Would the Beatles have been the *Beatles* without their keen competitive spirit? (That was a rhetorical question—the answer is clearly, no!) While it's not unheard of, it is rare for one rock band to have two leaders who are both so supremely talented at songwriting and singing and performing and playing multiple instruments and making the girls faint and winning over the universe with their wittiness and charm. It's amazing that two strong personalities with natural competitive instincts managed to collaborate so well.

In the early years of Beatlemania, Lennon and McCartney wrote songs "nose to nose" and "eyeball to eyeball," as Lennon put it. As time went on and more of their songs became distinctly Paul or John songs rather than full-on collaborations, they were inspired to one-up each other. For instance, when Lennon wrote "Strawberry Fields," McCartney wrote "Penny Lane," also a nostalgia-tinged song, in response.

And the competition surrounding some of the Beatles' songs wasn't limited to the confines of the band. When Brian Wilson, the "mad genius" of the Beach Boys, heard the Beatles' album *Rubber Soul*, it inspired him to make an album that would challenge him artistically and include more complex musical arrangements and harmonies than he'd used in the surfer songs the Beach Boys were best known for. The result was *Pet Sounds*, one of the most admired albums in rock history.

But that's not the end of the story. Before the record's release, Wilson played it for Lennon and McCartney, who listened to it in its entirety and then asked to hear it all over again. They began writing the groundbreaking *Sgt. Pepper's Lonely Hearts Club Band* almost immediately afterward. McCartney acknowledged that *Pet Sounds* ignited the competitive spirit in the Beatles and that the Beach Boys' experimentation made it seem possible for the Beatles to one-up their rivals. And, so, an appetite for competition, an A-Lister trait, is partly responsible for three of the greatest rock albums in history!

The street art world, too, is no stranger to competition. But not all competition has been friendly. In 1985, pioneering British street artist King Robbo painted what became known as the oldest lasting graffiti work in London, on a wall by a canal in the Camden section of London, accessible only by boat. Over time, British authorities, who considered his spray paintings vandalism rather than art, removed nearly all of them from the city's trains and walls but left the original piece standing.

And then street artist Banksy entered Robbo's life. The story goes that they met at a place called the Dragon Bar, and when they were introduced Banksy claimed he'd never heard of Robbo. In response, Robbo slapped him and said, "Oh, what, you ain't heard of me? You won't forget me now, will you!"

This interaction, which has become the stuff of legend, prompted an ongoing spat between the two artists. First, as captured in the documentary *Banksy vs. Robbo Graffiti Wars*, Banksy partially painted over Robbo's canal mural, provoking Robbo, who'd more or less "retired" from the street art world, into a comeback. Robbo altered Banksy's alteration of his own art by making it seem the workman that Banksy had depicted was painting "King Robbo." Three days later the letters *F-u-c* mysteriously appeared before the "King" (get it?).

The "war" continued until—and, in a sense, even after— Robbo suffered a sudden injury, probably caused by a fall that put him into a coma. He died shortly after, at the age of forty-four. In tribute to Robbo while he was still in a coma, Banksy returned to the Camden site and painted a black-and-white version of Robbo's original art with the additions of a crown and a can of spray paint with a hazard symbol of a flame above it. But then the mural was restored to its original form with slight changes by the other members of "Team Robbo." The restoration has since peeled away to leave the black-and-white tribute to Robbo, but who knows what the status of it will be by the time you read this.

Sure, the rivalry between Robbo and Banksy involved constant one-upmanship, repeated attempts by each to prove who was the alpha male, and an unabashed pursuit of publicity. It's not the purist reason to do art, but it brought Robbo out of retirement and into a bigger career, and it elevated Banksy's status. In the A-Listy world of street art, competition turned out well for both of them.

You'll probably find that your competitive nature can supply you with renewed determination when you're feeling stuck, creatively, or your confidence has taken a hit. For an A-Lister, competition is a motivation generator.

Creativity Booster
Naming Your Fears

A-Listers tend to appear self-confident, and, while some are, others hide their insecurities behind a mask of confidence. Putting your art—and yourself—out there in such characteristically big, A-Lister ways can be terrifying! The first step toward overcoming, or at least making peace with, your fears is identifying them. Some fears common to A-Listers are:

- Letting your ego get the better of you
- Worrying that success won't be as satisfying as you'd hoped
- Experiencing failure
- Seeing your popularity diminish, being forgotten, or having your art dismissed as no longer timely
- Losing out to competitors and upstarts

See which of these resonate with you, and think of three more fears to add to your list. Then, answer the question "What can I do?" for each one. For instance, if your worst fear as a director is that your play will close down after opening night, write about what you could do to accept this one failure and either move on or make changes to the play that would allow you to relaunch it at another theater. Repeat this exercise with your other fears, and see if it lessens the intensity of each one.

Cautionary Tales for the A-Lister

Ah, A-Listers, the same ego drive that fills you with brio and bravado is the very one that could make you super sensitive to any dip in attention or cause you to sacrifice your aesthetic ambitions for your fame-seeking ones. Let's look at some of the challenges you might face and consider which tendencies you can tame so you can achieve your dreams without them getting the better of you.

Valuing Product over Process

Dancer/choreographer Twyla Tharp, in her book *The Creative Habit*, presents a thought-provoking survey with thirty-three questions for readers to contemplate. My favorite is number 26: "When you work, do you love the process or the result?" When I pose this question to my students, many of them will try to wiggle out of it by answering "Both." But, if forced to choose, the A-Listers among them are likely to answer, "The result."

For an A-Lister, what's a greater ego thrill than seeing all your efforts finally come to fruition and then releasing your art into the world? Imagine this: walking by a bookstore and, *whoa*, there's your book with your name on it displayed dazzlingly in the window. Or saying your first line onstage after weeks of intense rehearsal. Or sitting in a movie theater with an audience who's watching your movie—*your* movie—on a ginormous screen.

Imagining your moment of "making it" can keep you going, especially during the rough patches: when you're not seeing eye-to-eye with your dance partner or you're feeling like you can't possibly reach the required word count or you're worried that if you haven't succeeded by now, you're never going to. Chances are, you *will* make it, if you can keep that moment before you, a North Star to your creative longings.

Tame Your Tendencies
Learning to Appreciate the Process

If you're the kind of A-Lister who has your eye on the prize (adoration, commercial success, etc.) instead of the process, here's a question worth pondering: What sort of artistic projects would you be doing if you weren't concerned with audience reaction, critics, or fame? Once you've answered that question, try to set aside time on a regular basis to "fool around" on the piano or in the dance studio, without any goals other than enjoying yourself. It will remind you how much fun it is to make art for its own sake.

But, here's a word of caution, A-Lister: being laser-focused on the end results has its upsides, but research reveals (as you'll see in Chapter 2, "The Artisan") it has its downsides, too. For one, you could lose your enjoyment of the process if you treat it as something to "get through" just so you can receive the grand acclaim and financial rewards you desire. Also, when you're more ambitious about achieving success than you are about doing good work, your art can suffer—and isn't the art what matters most?

Great Expectations Aren't Always So Great

Some A-Listers act against their own best interests by thinking they'll only be satisfied if they're superstars (not stars), the play's lead (not a supporting actor), a best-selling author (not a mid-list author), and so on. Imagining yourself at the top of your field can be motivating, but it can also be paralyzing to the point at which you fail to create anything at all.

Think about times when you may have fallen into this trap. Maybe you've thought or even said things aloud like this: "If I can't get a good record deal, I'm just not going to sing anymore." (That's showing 'em.) Or, "What's the point of making movies when I'll never be as good as Wes Anderson?" (The "why bother" school of film.) Or, "I can't believe I put so much effort into it and the show didn't sell out. Don't people recognize true talent anymore?" ("A" for effort doesn't exist.) Or, "Why would anybody care about my life?" (What if popular memoirists Elizabeth Gilbert, Mary Karr, or Cheryl Strayed had let that deter them?)

A-Lister, these thoughts might be masking a fear of success, a fear of failure—or both. You might have been raised to think creative pursuits are only appropriate as hobbies, not as a "real job," and so you're under pressure to prove yourself as a self-sufficient artist. Or, maybe you were told by your mom and your drama teacher that you're uniquely talented, and so you've been set up to believe you deserve to be cast in nothing less than the next Lin-Manuel Miranda play. It's exhausting to yo-yo between hyped-up expectations and fears of never reaching them.

Cheryl Strayed addressed this paradoxical attitude in one of the letters she wrote for her "Dear Sugar" advice column for the online magazine The Rumpus. She was responding to a young woman who feared she'd never manage to overcome her limitations and become the sort of writer she dreamed of being. Strayed could tell this woman was suffering from the enormous pressure she was placing on herself, the sort of pressure that demonstrates the A-Lister's proclivity toward being, as Strayed called it, "up too high and down too low."

And so Strayed explained how, in order to write her first book, the novel Torch, she had to learn humility. She writes, "I had to write my book. My very possibly mediocre book. My very possibly never-going-to-be-published book. My absolutely nowhere-in-league-with-the-writers-I'd-admired-so-much-that-I-practically-memorized their sentences book. It was only then, when I humbly surrendered, that I was able to do the work I needed to do." And, she ended her letter with one of my all-time favorite lines of advice: "Write like a motherfucker."

Control Freakiness

Famed director Alfred Hitchcock once said, "In the fiction film, the director is the god; he must create life." Some A-Listers think of themselves as akin to gods—and, in a way, they are. Aren't all creative people? While you probably don't parade around like Hitchcock or Pablo Picasso (as you'll see in the Spotlight), announcing you *are* God, you might enjoy *playing* God. This sentiment may be especially true for writers—whether novelists, screenwriters, playwrights, or others—who invent characters and then determine their fate, moving them here or there, marrying them off to the wrong people, placing them at the front lines of a war, or inventing myriad other obstacles to their happiness.

Be aware, dear A-Lister, that this wish to construct a world of your own making may reflect a desire for control, the sort of dictatorial power over people and situations that eludes you in real life. Channeling your desire for control into your art may be healthy, but there might be a price to pay for assuming such godlike powers.

The movie *The Hours*, based on the novel of the same name by Michael Cunningham, captures this nearly Machiavellian obsession some writers have with manipulating the lives of fictional characters. We see the character of the esteemed writer Virginia Woolf (played by Nicole Kidman in an Academy Award–winning performance) writing the classic modernist novel *Mrs. Dalloway*. As she's contemplating the story and the various characters whose lives she gets to manipulate, she muses aloud about her protagonist Clarissa Dalloway, "She'll die. She's going to die. That's what's going to happen. She'll kill herself. She'll kill herself over something which doesn't seem to matter." As becomes clear to the viewer, this is probably also the filmmaker's reference to the death of Woolf herself, who committed suicide in 1941 by filling her coat pockets with heavy stones and wading into the River Ouse to drown.

But later in the film, Woolf experiences a jolt of clarity. While her beloved sister Vanessa and Vanessa's children are visiting her at her home in a London suburb, Woolf is lost in thought. When Vanessa asks what's on her mind, Woolf replies, "I was going to kill my heroine. But I've changed my mind. I can't. And then I'll have to kill someone else instead." And she does.

While the fictionalized Woolf has no qualms about her godlike role in determining the fate of her characters, humorist Fran Lebowitz feels otherwise. Lebowitz grew up believing writing was a godly act. She said in a *Paris Review* interview, "When I was very little, say five or six, I became aware of the fact that people wrote books. Before that, I thought that God wrote books. I thought a book was a manifestation of nature, like a tree. When my mother explained it, I kept after her: What are you saying? What do you mean? I couldn't believe it. It was astonishing. It was like—here's the man who makes all the trees. Then I wanted to be a writer, because, I suppose, it seemed the closest thing to being God."

Is it presumptuous to be a creator? Lebowitz thinks so—and she believes this can induce guilt. In Martin Scorsese's documentary about her, *Public Speaking*, Lebowitz says, "The history of writing is... when people are actually writing they are doing something bad to themselves at the same time. People used to drink, people smoked. While you're writing, you're doing something bad to yourself, and that is to punish yourself for playing God."

The idea of having to "atone" for the sin of writing fiction based on people's lives is also at the heart of the novel *Atonement* by Ian McEwan. In it, a thirteen-year-old girl, Briony, misunderstands the interaction she's witnessed between her sister and a suitor and turns her misperceptions into a short story, much to the detriment of their love and their lives. After she grows up and comes to understand the full implications of her actions, Briony asks, "How can a novelist achieve atonement when, with her absolute power of deciding outcomes, she is also God?" The somewhat ironic answer in Briony's case is that she was fated to spend a lifetime writing her novel as a means of making up for her past sins.

These concerns about an author's power is reminiscent of the Greek myth of Icarus, in which Icarus's father crafted wings for him from feathers and wax but warned him against the hubris of thinking he could fly close to the sun. Naturally, he did and his wings melted and he ended up drowning in the sea.

Is it hubris to create? To fly so close to the sun? Probably. Nevertheless, divine aspiration (not just inspiration) can be a driving force for A-Listers. While it may cause some hand-wringing, in most cases playing God doesn't harm others and allows you to design a world of your own making, immerse yourself in your imagination, and play out life-and-death scenarios in fiction that would be devastating in real life.

Spotlight: Pablo Picasso, An Ego Unbound

There's a reason so many creative superstars possess A-Lister traits and tendencies. A powerful ego, which is the beating heart of the A-Lister, isn't merely important for creativity; it's essential.

And, so, use those great reserves of ego to pursue your passion but also be aware of how a strong ego can become an ego unbound... as in the case of **Pablo Picasso**.

Picasso is considered one of—if not *the*—most prolific and influential artists of the twentieth century. And, he was recognized as such during his long life—no toiling away in obscurity for him! I'm not here to tell you his enormous ego was detrimental to his painting. But, if you want to be the sort of A-Lister who is ambitious and accomplished and is also regarded as a decent person, read this as a cautionary tale.

Like most A-Listers, one key to Picasso's success was his lack of ambivalence about achieving it. As he told the famous photographer Brassaï, considered "the eye of Paris" in the 1930s, "Success is an important thing! It's often been said that an artist ought to work for himself, for the 'love of art,' that he ought to have contempt for success. Untrue! An artist needs success. And not only to live off it, but especially to produce his body of work." But Picasso also believed an artist must stay true to himself, saying, "Where is it written that success must always go to those who cater to the public's taste? For myself, I wanted to prove that you can have success in spite of everyone, without compromise."

Picasso's incomparable drive did not come without consequences. According to multiple accounts from those who knew him and from art historians, Picasso's ego—and cruelty—were limitless. Paul Johnson, in his book *Creators*, offers alternately amusing and frightening accounts of Picasso's overweening ego. Did you know, for instance, that long before Richard Nixon's enemies list, Picasso kept one, which contained, among others, the names of anyone who befriended the "other" Cubist, Georges Braque? As for painter and pal Henri Matisse, Picasso dismissed his whimsical art with jabs like, "What is a Matisse? A balcony with a big red flowerpot falling over it." Juan Gris, a painter and sculptor and fellow Spaniard, suffered more than verbal barbs from Picasso. Picasso convinced patrons to drop Gris, tried to prevent him from getting commissions, and then, when he died young, feigned grief.

But, wait, there's more! Picasso's most famous romantic partner, Françoise Gilot, left him and later wrote a book about their lives in which she claimed that Picasso divided women into "goddesses and doormats" and boasted that his object was to turn the goddess into the doormat. She also claimed that Picasso told her, "I would rather see a woman die than see her happy with someone else."

He apparently didn't want to see other men happy, either, not even his own son. After Gilot told Picasso she was going to publish her memoir, he banned his children with her, Claude and Paloma, from ever seeing him again. He was eighty-two, had presumably lost his sexual potency, and reportedly said to Claude the last time he saw him, "I am old and you are young. I wish you were dead."

And here's the coup de grace: Picasso once insisted to a friend, "God is really another artist… like me… I am God, I am God, I am God." It's hard to top that for egocentric proclamations!

There's no denying Picasso got what A-Listers often desire: fame, money, sexual attention, immortality through art, and an everlasting place in the pantheon of art "greats." But at what personal cost to himself and those around him?

Tame Your Tendencies
Check Your Ego at the Door

A-Lister, you've got to admit you can sometimes get a little carried away with your ambitions and desires and angling for the spotlight, right? So, here's a mantra you can say to yourself whenever you feel your control over your ego slipping away: "Don't let my ego get the better of me. Don't let my ego get the better of me. Don't let my ego get the better of me." Now, doesn't that feel good?

The Student Outmasters the Teacher

In Chapter 2 you'll see how Artisans admire and honor their artistic predecessors. A-Listers, too, are in thrall to their artistic idols, but some just can't wait to outdo them. They're plagued by the feeling that until they slay the giant that looms so large, they haven't "made it." While this ambition is clearly motivating to an A-Lister, it presents certain issues, too, as with painters Jackson Pollock and Pablo Picasso.

Painting was long considered a European art form, and even by the mid-twentieth century, no American painter had emerged from the long, sometimes oppressive shadow cast by Picasso in particular. That is, until Pollock took him on. Pollock's wife, painter Lee Krasner, described her husband's relationship with Picasso by saying he admired and yet competed with him and wanted to exceed him. Krasner once recalled, "I remember one time I heard something fall and then Jackson yelling, 'God damn it, that guy missed nothing!' I went to see what had happened. Jackson was sitting, staring; and on the floor, where he had thrown it, was a book of Picasso's work."

The biopic *Pollock* shows the painter in an alcoholic rage when Picasso's name is mentioned (although, in fairness, he was often shown in an alcoholic rage when Picasso's name *wasn't* mentioned). He even began a 1950 drip painting with a series of Picasso-like figures but then buried them under layers of paint—that's how much of a daunting influence the famous artist once had on the emerging one.

But, emerge he did, with the distinct splatter technique he invented that revolutionized the world of abstract expressionist painting and placed America on the art world map. His ascendancy was announced in a four-page spread in the August 8, 1949, issue of *Life* magazine with his name in big block letters and the provocative question placed under it: "Is he the greatest living painter in the United States?" It put the world on notice that here was a painter to be reckoned with. And this was due in no small part to Pollock's desire to dethrone Picasso.

And yet, Pollock's newfound success brought him only temporary satisfaction and didn't solve his apparent personality problems or rampant alcoholism, which ultimately caused the car accident that killed him and his young lover's friend. If Pollock was *so* motivated by outdoing what some have referred to as his "Oedipal father," wasn't his success in that regard a pyrrhic victory?

Another potential scenario in trying to overtake your idol is that the idol may not take so kindly to the challenge, which appears to be an issue for singers Lady Gaga and Madonna. In 2008, when Gaga released her first album, *The Fame*, critics and music fans alike took notice of the similarities between her and Madonna. Some criticized Gaga for imitating Madonna's music style, attire, and sexuality. And when Gaga released the song "Born This Way" in 2011, it prompted a feud between the two divas, with Madonna and some others claiming Gaga's song sounded strikingly similar to Madonna's song "Express Yourself."

In an interview with Howard Stern, Gaga dismissed the comparison, saying, "It's silly. There's always this pissing match, 'Did she take her torch?' 'Is she the new her?' 'Is she going to outlast her?' There's this thing with some people that I'm a threat to the throne, and I don't want your f—ing throne and no thanks. And I have my own and I don't actually want a throne at all."

For her part, in 2012 during a world tour, Madonna sang a mash-up of "Express Yourself" and "Born This Way" to prove the similarities between the songs. While the feud does seem petty, it's got to be a little unnerving to a superstar to witness a younger version of herself on the ascent. But, as an A-Lister, it's a reality you may need to learn to accept someday.

Remaining Relevant

Nothing strikes fear into an A-Lister's heart like the threat of becoming irrelevant, but the arts are a fickle business. As Heidi Klum cautions the fashion design competitors on the television show *Project Runway*, "As you know, in fashion one day you're in and the next day you're out." Harsh! It's true in all artistic fields, though, especially those that value youth and trendiness.

When novelist Toni Morrison conducted a wide-ranging interview with her friend Fran Lebowitz, they discussed the topic of youth and creativity. Lebowitz noted that writers who "specialize in youth" are destined to have short careers and pointed to F. Scott Fitzgerald as a cautionary tale. Not only did Fitzgerald immerse himself in and write about a world of youthful excess, he died young, at the age of forty-four. (Of course, many of us would trade a long career for a short one that boasted a novel as admired as *The Great Gatsby*.)

Novelist Philip Roth, by contrast, has published two breakthrough books *and* achieved decades of admired output. He established himself in 1959 with the novella and story collection *Goodbye, Columbus* and cemented his reputation as a literary light with 1969's *Portnoy's Complaint*, which has made many lists of best novels. The protagonists of these books were indeed young, but as Roth aged his characters got older, too, and the concerns he explored expanded. He produced multiple novels over the course of several decades. Many won prestigious awards, including the Pulitzer Prize and the National Book Award, and some were adapted for film. And he even became a hero to the AARP set by experiencing a renaissance of sorts in his seventies, when he produced novel after novel, including many of his most acclaimed ones.

Still, Roth has struggled with issues of relevance, trying and failing to retire from writing more than once and predicting that, with people's dwindling attention spans, reading novels will become a cultish activity, not engaged in by most people. And so, even an author who's defied the odds by achieving sustained popularity fears he'll become irrelevant to the culture.

For performers, whose careers are so often tied to their youthful appeal and physicality, the fear of becoming irrelevant looms even larger. The 2014 film *Birdman or (The Unexpected Virtue of Ignorance)* captured this dread so viscerally. The movie is about a fading actor's bid for artistic significance again after attaining and losing pop culture glory playing Birdman in the superhero film franchise.

The actor, Riggan Thomson (played by Michael Keaton, who received a Golden Globe for Best Actor—Motion Picture Musical or Comedy), hopes to reawaken his career by writing, directing, and starring in a Broadway production of a loosely based adaptation of Raymond Carver's story, "What We Talk About When We Talk About Love." He tells his daughter Sam, "This is my chance to do some work that actually means something."

Sam responds with a verbal thrashing that makes the gap in "generation gap" feel more like a chasm. With her eyes bugging out and spit nearly spraying from her mouth, she eviscerates her father: "You're doing this because you're scared to death, like the rest of us, that you don't matter. And you know what? You're right. You don't. It's not important, okay? You're not important. Get used to it!"

But, if you're an A-Lister, and especially if you're a Baby Boomer A-Lister, you don't want to get used to it, and you won't leave center stage unless you're forced to. This is reminiscent of the old days at the Apollo Theater in Harlem, when Sandman Sims, the celebrated tap dancer and Apollo mainstay, would be called upon to act as "executioner" and chase an awful performer offstage or even drag him or her off with a hook. Unfortunately, a metaphorical hook with the same purpose isn't reserved only for the untalented; it's also used on talented actors, ballet dancers, comedians, and other performers as they age.

This can be a hard reckoning for A-Listers, not just because you may not get to continue doing what you love or earn a living at it but also because rejection based on a reality you can't control is a terrible, terrible blow—especially if you've had decades of success. But take heart! There are some valuable lessons to learn from performers who've overcome the odds against longevity in the arts, as you'll see in the Spotlight.

Spotlight: Timeless Performers

Certain performers have the knack for doing work, decade after decade, that allows them to hold on to their loyal fan base while also attracting new, young admirers. Here are some standouts:

Lucinda Williams is a singer-songwriter best known for 1998's *Car Wheels on a Gravel Road*, an album that went gold and won Williams her second Grammy and universal acclaim by music critics. While Williams isn't a stadium headliner, she's got hardcore fans; has toured with Bob Dylan, the Allman Brothers, and Tom Petty and the Heartbreakers; and was named "America's Best Songwriter" by *Time* magazine in 2001.

What I most admire about Williams is how she's consistently produced new songs that reflect where she is in her life as she ages and her experiences have deepened. On her most recent albums, for every song about love and lust, there's one about spirituality or coming to terms with loss, such as the death of her beloved father, the poet Miller Williams. In fact, the 2014 album *Down Where the Spirit Meets the Bone* kicks off with the song "Compassion," in which Williams put her father's poetry to music.

In an interview on NPR, Williams acknowledged that the label "veteran singer-songwriter" was a little disconcerting because she doesn't feel her age, which was sixty-one at the time, and because her songwriting seems to keep getting stronger. She said, "Most artists create their best work early on and they just kind of fizzle out, and I seem to be doing the opposite." Williams attributed her unflagging creativity to her strong drive and to the realities of life as you age, saying, "The more loss and pain you experience, the more you need your art."

Williams has a long way to go to match the longevity of vocalist **Tony Bennett**, who, as of this writing, is selling records and filling venues at the age of ninety. As Bennett got older, his son and manager, Danny, booked his father on late night shows to reach a young audience and encouraged him to do music videos that would play on MTV. That was the start of his revitalized career, which has made him a hit with a new generation of music lovers. Bennett also produced albums of duets performed with singers decades younger. Lady Gaga, for one, collaborated with him on the 2014 album *Cheek to Cheek*, which featured songs by popular jazz composers such as Cole Porter, George Gershwin, Jerome Kern, and Irving Berlin. It was, as they say, a win-win: Gaga made it clear she wanted to be taken more seriously as a vocalist, and she introduced Bennett to her extensive young fan base.

Bennett told *The New York Times* he has no intention of retiring and, instead, wants to emulate the careers of Pablo Picasso, comedian Jack Benny, and dancer Fred Astaire. He said, "Right up to the day they died, they were performing. If you are creative, you get busier as you get older."

Jane Fonda knows exactly what Bennett was talking about. This two-time Academy Award–winning actress, model, activist, fitness guru, writer, daughter of acclaimed actor Henry Fonda, and ex-wife of business magnate Ted Turner is seventy-eight as of this writing and starring with Lily Tomlin in one of Netflix's most successful original series, *Grace and Frankie*. It must be exhausting to be Jane! She's managed to stay relevant and driven for over five decades by continually reinventing herself. While her daughter calls her a chameleon, Fonda says she's simply curious, and her curiosity has led her to try new things and, in the process, become a cultural weathervane for so many decades.

Fonda's continuing success has much to do with her never-say-die attitude. As she told *The Washington Post*, "What matters is realizing you can always get better. That you have to keep taking leaps of faith. It gets harder as you get older. You have to stay brave and keep trying to go beyond your comfort zone and see what you need to get to become who you're supposed to be." And she asks herself, "How can I remain an interested and full person who is relevant?"

Like Fonda, **Meryl Streep** hopes she can change Hollywood's harshness toward actresses who are middle-aged and older. Despite Streep's oft-repeated reputation as "the greatest actress of her generation," she struggled to find a footing and receive worthy roles when she reached her fifties. But, she also saw this setback as an opportunity to shift from serious dramatic parts to comedic roles. They are usually based on strong-willed women, such as in *The Devil Wears Prada*, in which Streep portrays a character presumably based on the feared editor in chief of *Vogue*, Anna Wintour, and *Julie & Julia*, where she plays beloved chef Julia Child. Streep emphasized the importance of making choices that are right for you, saying in a *Vanity Fair* interview, "As there begins to be less time ahead of you, you want to be exactly who you are, without making it easier for everyone else."

If you're an A-Lister who's been in the arts for a long time and is struggling to overcome ageism, you can also look to the actress and wit (and daughter of Debbie Reynolds and Eddie Fisher) **Carrie Fisher** for how to have the last laugh. Fisher, forever linked (one

Nurture Your Tendencies
Remain Relevant

No A-Lister can tolerate being kicked to the curb because times have changed or they've gotten a little older. So, here are some strategies for continuing to matter to the culture for a long time:

- Choose an artistic field that is more behind-the-scenes to begin with, one that's not so ageist.
- Be careful at the start of your career about taking on roles or projecting a persona that is all about being young and hot.
- Over time, seek opportunities to shift from being front and center to more behind the scenes, such as from acting to directing or from dancing to doing choreography.
- If you're a writer, start addressing more mature topics and developing characters with complex life experiences that reflect your own.
- No matter what field you're in, "pay it forward" by teaching and mentoring young people.
- And, most of all, try, dear A-Lister, to be grateful for your moment in the sun and never, ever take it for granted.

might say handcuffed) to her iconic role as Princess Leia in *Star Wars*, was criticized by Internet trolls for having the nerve to look her age in 2015's *Star Wars: The Force Awakens*, almost forty years after she appeared in the original movie. In response to the cruel remarks, she sent a six-word tweet that could serve as a manifesto for aging A-Listers everywhere: "Youth is temporary, diva is forever."

The Takeaway

If you're an A-Lister or someone with A-Lister tendencies, you're ambitious as all get-out, are vulnerable to what others think, and feel most alive in the spotlight.

What can you do to make the most of your egoistic drive while not allowing it to compromise your artistic spirit?

- Watch out for too much pride—it's a great motivator, but it could also be your Achilles' heel.
- An artist's income is unpredictable, and fame, as they say, is fleeting. So, even if these motivate you at the start, figure out what will keep you going in the long run.
- Be a bully… but only the artistic kind.
- Keep in mind that there's such a thing as collaboration or "friendly" competition (it worked pretty well for the Beatles).
- Learn to love the creative process as much as the product.
- Try to stay true to yourself and your art. Don't let commercial pressures or fear of losing your popularity force you off course.

Chapter 2

THE ARTISAN: TRULY, MADLY, DEEPLY DEVOTED TO CREATIVITY

ᴗᴗᴗ

I know nothing in the world that has as much power as a word.
Sometimes I write one, and I look at it, until it begins to shine.

—EMILY DICKINSON

Are you the bass player in the band? A cinematographer? How about a playwright? You appreciate applause, adulation, and ac-claim, but you don't necessarily want to be the star. You don't need a lot of outside validation, and you don't live for it. Just being cre-ative is its own satisfaction.

When you're writing and you find exactly the right word—not one that's close or good enough but *exactly the right word*—does this make you happy beyond reason?

Maybe you get so absorbed in sculpting or knitting that you lose all sense of time or place—or people.

When your manuscript is completed or postproduction on a film is done, are you excited but also sad because you won't get to keep working on this beloved project?

You just might be an Artisan.

Why Do Artisans Create?

If you're an Artisan or you have Artisan tendencies, you're drawn to the creative process the way a beagle's drawn to food: too much can never be enough. It's both sustenance and addiction. And so, you'll probably relate to a lot of these reasons for creating.

You create because you love making something from nothing—it never ceases to amaze you. Because you can't imagine your life without this outlet, this escape, this joy. Because when your parents gave you your first guitar on your ninth birthday, it beckoned to you as a lighthouse signals to a sailor that he's home at last. Because you've found an activity that absorbs you and keeps your mind from spinning in circles. Because your first novel got mixed reviews and the bad ones hurt—let's be honest—but they didn't defeat you, they didn't ruin you. Because you don't care much for material things (which is good, since most artists don't make a lot of money). Because you find inspiration all around you: in nature, in people, in the artists and art that have left their mark on you. Because being an artist can be a pretty lonely existence, but it doesn't have to be for you. You enjoy collaboration, and so you've got your bandmates, your castmates, your coauthor, or your lyricist to challenge you, inspire you, and keep you going.

Snapshot of an Artisan

Artisans worship at the altar of Art, and to them there's no worthier deity.

If you're an Artisan, for every poem you send out for publication, there are one hundred more that will never see the light of day. Why would you waste your time tracking down the right editor when you could be writing? After all, getting published isn't the most important reason for writing poetry—not to an Artisan.

Artistic Personality Quiz
So, You Think You're an Artisan

1. Do you geek out over the best chord change, the perfect interface for your app, or the right texture of fabric?
2. Would you keep making art even if no one paid attention to it—or money *for* it?
3. Do you sometimes become so immersed in your work that you lose all sense of time, place, and people?
4. Do you love the creative process even more than the finished product?
5. Could you be satisfied with a modest lifestyle—no mansion, no infinity pool, no fleet of cars, no car at all—as long as you had what you needed to do creative work?
6. Do you think you'd have found a creative outlet even if you weren't given encouragement or lessons or, worse, were told you weren't entitled to pursue your passion?
7. Do you believe creativity is something like nine parts perspiration and one part inspiration?
8. Are you grateful for the artists who came before you, influenced you, and even paved the way for you?
9. Are you eager to sometimes collaborate with others rather than to always fly solo?

If you answered "yes" to most of these questions, you are an Artisan. And, if you answered "yes" to even a few of these questions, you have strong Artisan tendencies. Either way, read on.

Artisans know one thing for sure about themselves: they'd do the work they love whether or not they received any compensation for it or even any acknowledgment by others that it exists. Or that *they* exist.

If you're an Artisan, here's one of your favorite kinds of morning: you wake up, and the answer to a creative problem you've been wrestling with for days is suddenly clear, as if it came to you in a dream. You race to your easel, desk, or studio and get down to business. Sound familiar? The telephone's buzzing? The doorbell's ringing? Someone's tapping you on the shoulder? You're so absorbed, you won't even notice.

But, sharing a sublet with roommates and forgoing financial security in the name of art may seem dreamy at twenty but not so much at forty. And now and then you can't help but think, "How come Ms. Self-Promotion got a one-woman gallery show and no one even knows who I am?"

Take heart, Artisan. You've got what a lot of other people wish for: a true passion for creativity and an unwavering ability to get the job done.

Varieties of Artisans

You might be the kind of Artisan who lives in your head, ignoring the conversation around you while you figure out the best lighting for the opening scene of a new play. You might be the sort of Artisan who seems to be living la dolce vita when, really, you'd rather be hanging out at home fooling around on your guitar, coming up with an unforgettable hook.

See the Sidebar for a list of varieties of Artisans, and read on for an exploration of some of the most common ones.

Revenge of the Nerds

There was a time not so very long ago when being called a nerd or geek was not meant as a compliment (during my childhood, for instance). But today, it's cool to be a nerd. This is good news for

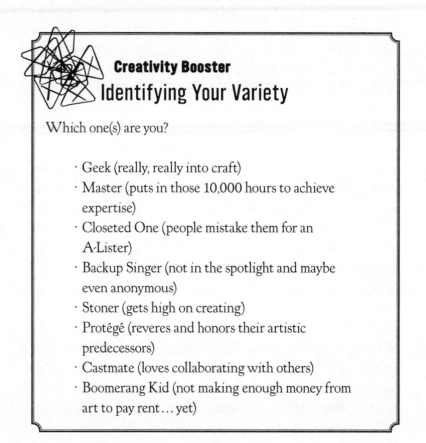

Creativity Booster
Identifying Your Variety

Which one(s) are you?

- Geek (really, really into craft)
- Master (puts in those 10,000 hours to achieve expertise)
- Closeted One (people mistake them for an A-Lister)
- Backup Singer (not in the spotlight and maybe even anonymous)
- Stoner (gets high on creating)
- Protégé (reveres and honors their artistic predecessors)
- Castmate (loves collaborating with others)
- Boomerang Kid (not making enough money from art to pay rent... yet)

Artisans, who love to delve into the tools and craft of their art. Your creative work will reflect your attention to detail and your eagerness to learn and perfect new techniques. So, Artisan, feel free to let your geek flag fly!

You can take inspiration from a couple of famous artists who are renowned for their dedication to getting it right—some might say to the point of obsession.

Guitar gods admire U2's The Edge for using innovative technology that makes his electric guitar playing sound unlike anyone else's in rock stardom. In the documentary *It Might Get Loud*, this is how he describes his discovery of distortion, which sent him down the road to guitar geekdom: "I just got totally into playing but listening to the return echo, filling in notes that I'm not play-ing, like two guitar players rather than one. The exact same thing but just a little bit off to one side. I could see ways to use it that had never been used. Suddenly, everything changed."

Distortion was just the first of The Edge's many technological discoveries. In fact, on at least one of U2's mega-concert tours, not a single sound on one song repeated on any other song, thanks to his endless experimentation. The Edge wouldn't have it any other way. As he told *Guitar World*, "Just as a comedian doesn't want to tell the same jokes over and over, we don't want to play the same songs the same way."

Another artist with this Artisan tendency of obsessive at-tention to detail is Daniel Day-Lewis. While he's well known as a Method actor, the full extent to which he dedicates himself to each role might surprise you. "Films don't begin only when the cam-era starts rolling," he told *The Telegraph*. Before playing Christy Brown, a real-life writer and artist with cerebral palsy, in the movie *My Left Foot*, Day-Lewis spent eight weeks at a cerebral palsy clinic. While there, he learned to speak and paint with his left foot as Brown had done. During the movie's production, he stayed in character, never leaving his wheelchair. The crew fed him and helped him maneuver over the cables on set.

As Hawkeye in *The Last of the Mohicans*, Day-Lewis learned how to build canoes, fight with tomahawks, and track and skin an-imals. He also carried his gun, a 12-pound flintlock, everywhere. When he played the title role in Steven Spielberg's *Lincoln*, he insisted on being addressed as "Mr. President," signed messages as "Abe," and spoke with Lincoln's accent both on and off-screen. Could this degree of dedication be responsible for Day-Lewis's three Oscars for Best Actor? Indeed.

The Master

Artisans don't tend to be dabblers. Once they commit to an art form, they want to become experts at it and are willing to put in the necessary time. And it turns out that time and practice are more essential to success at the arts than was previously thought.

Malcolm Gladwell, in his book *Outliers*, popularized the 10,000-hour rule, which proposes that the key to achieving world-class expertise in any skill is largely a matter of practicing the correct way for approximately 10,000 hours. As an example, Gladwell points to the experience gained by the Beatles during their gigs at strip clubs in Hamburg, Germany, from 1960 through the end of 1962. Before that defining experience, the Beatles had only played one-hour sessions of their best material at Liverpool clubs where the crowd was "their" crowd. But in Hamburg, where they performed for 270 nights in just over a year and a half, they sometimes played five hours a night. They had to learn new material and try out new ways of winning over a foreign audience who spoke a different language. As music historian Philip Norman observed in *Shout! The Beatles in Their Generation*, "They weren't disciplined at all before [Hamburg]. But when they came back, they sounded like no one else. It was the making of them."

By the time the Beatles appeared on the *Ed Sullivan Show* a little over a year later in February 1964, charming in their matching suits and mop-top haircuts, they had performed live an estimated 1,200 times. That's more than most bands perform their entire careers!

Talented from the start? Yeah, yeah, yeah. But, in their case, brilliant natural talent + nonstop practice = mastery.

Think about how this is true for you, Artisan. You might have started out really young, let's say at four or five, as *that* kid—the one who could draw circles around the other kids (literally) or write stories that captivated your classmates or do the Michael Jackson moonwalk without a hitch. You stood out for your natural abilities in the arts. But, it's the years—even decades—of hours spent in the studio, on the laptop, or on the dance floor that have elevated you to where you are today or where you're headed in the future.

The Closeted One

Sometimes an artist who's living large like an A-Lister may not be quite as A-Listy as you'd think. In fact, he or she might even be a secret Artisan or at least have a lot of Artisan qualities. Maybe you can relate: you've got the A-Lister's dream of owning a beach house bought with your royalties, no one would ever call you shy or retiring, and you post on social media more often than you'd care to admit. Yet, in true Artisan style, your greatest satisfaction comes when you're doing something creative.

If that describes you, you have something in common with Rolling Stones guitarist Keith Richards.

When people think of Richards, what usually comes to mind is the caricature of a hard-drinking, drugging, smoking, word-slurring, cackling, craggy-looking former bad boy of rock 'n' roll. Yet, when you hear Richards talk (if you can understand what he's saying), you realize this is a man whose most affecting, most enduring addiction is, simply put, the blues.

One day in 1961, Richards was on a train when he suddenly spotted his childhood chum Mick Jagger carrying two albums under his arm, *The Best of Muddy Waters* and Chuck Berry's *Rockin' at the Hops*. It was, to paraphrase the line from the movie *Casablanca*, "the start of a beautiful [renewed] friendship." It was also the start of a phenomenon much larger than the two of them. As Richards recalls in the documentary *Keith Richards: Under the Influence*, "I thought I was the only guy in the southeast of

England that knew anything about this stuff." He was thrilled to learn he was wrong.

Their mutual passion for the blues is what led Jagger and Richards to form what would become one of the greatest rock bands in history. The band even took its name from a song on the Muddy Waters LP called "Rollin' Stone," and songs from both albums, including Muddy Water's "I Just Want to Make Love to You" and Berry's "Let It Rock," would have a place on their set lists for decades to come. Richards has made a point of honoring the blues players he adores and who, it must be said, never received anything near the financial compensation the Stones have. He looks blissful, egoless in those moments when he's accompanying his idols onstage.

Yet Richards claims the stage is not where he most wants to be, at least not now in his seventies: "My idea of actual heaven is to be a rock and roll star that nobody ever sees... totally anonymous. But you gotta go out and do this thing sometimes."

That might sound disingenuous. After all, these are the words of a man who's already gotten to live "the life" and wouldn't have had it any other way. But Richards sure sounded sincere when he made that very Artisan-like statement.

Who's That Girl?

You know when you see a work of art, such as a quilt hanging at a museum, signed by "Anonymous" or "Anon," circa 1864? Such pieces were usually produced by women or African Americans or other people who did not have societal status. So, they didn't sign their work, or, in the case of some women, they used a male pseudonym to help get their novel published or their art hung on a museum wall.

An A-Lister or Game Changer might wonder, how could these artists stand not to receive any credit or recognition or money?

Why did they continue to create, knowing full well that their work would bear the "Anonymous" mark instead of their name? Well, this is one of the qualities that differentiates an Artisan from some of the other creative types: the Artisan will soldier on even without external validation or rewards.

It's disturbing to consider how many of the famous artists we now revere toiled in obscurity, whether out of choice or necessity. So, let's hear it for the women artists, in particular, who demonstrated incredible persistence despite the initial lack of acclaim.

Jane Austen was not widely read or known in her time, the late eighteenth and early nineteenth centuries; few people even attended her funeral. She published her novels anonymously and only members of the aristocracy knew she was the author. Her books received little critical praise, although they were considered "fashionable." Audiences preferred the writings of George Eliot, a woman who took on a male pseudonym, and Charles Dickens.

But at the time of the Industrial Revolution, audiences began warming to Austen, and during World War I her books provided solace to soldiers in the trenches. This remained true as well in World War II, when no less a luminary than Winston Churchill quipped, "Antibiotics and Jane Austen got me through the war." It took until then for Austen to achieve not only popularity but also critical recognition, although to this day she's dismissed by some as "just" a writer of domestic affairs or as the originator of "chick lit," a pejorative label at best. Of course, a new generation has come to know her not just through her novels but also through popular movies based on *Pride and Prejudice, Sense and Sensibility,* and others; the current-day novels and movies inspired by them, including the *Bridget Jones* series; and, well, the zombie versions, too.

Emily Dickinson published fewer than a dozen poems during her lifetime, and even those were edited to fit the traditional styles of the nineteenth century. Most of her poetry was published posthumously after her sister Lavinia discovered a cache of nearly eighteen hundred poems. Did you catch that number? *Eighteen hundred!* Dickinson's poems did not always garner positive reviews among the early critics, with Thomas Bailey Aldrich writing in *The Atlantic Monthly* that "an eccentric, dreamy, half-educated recluse in an out-of-the-way New England village (or anywhere else) cannot with impunity set at defiance the laws of gravitation and grammar." It took a few decades for the literary world to realize the brilliance of her gravity-defying poems.

Going years without recognition is not only a common challenge for female Artisans of centuries past. Bettye LaVette, dubbed "the best soul singer nobody knows," released her first album in 1962 at age sixteen. The single "My Man—He's a Lovin' Man" even made it to the top ten on the R&B chart. At first it seemed that LaVette was only a flash in the pan. Not so! Decades later, when she was nearly sixty, she reemerged as a noteworthy singer when she released the 2005 album *I've Got My Own Hell to Raise.* She's since shared the stage with the likes of Paul McCartney and Bon Jovi. LaVette has also been nominated for and won prestigious music awards, including the 2008 Blues Music Award for "Best Contemporary Female Blues Singer." Listen to her song "Before the Money Came," and you'll understand how it felt to live under the radar for so many decades.

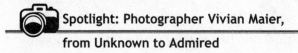 **Spotlight: Photographer Vivian Maier,**

from Unknown to Admired

Imagine taking more than 150,000 photographs during your lifetime and not showing them to others—not even developing thousands of them? (I'm talking before smartphones, before the digital age, when film needed to be developed with chemicals.) That's what street photographer **Vivian Maier** did. Surprisingly, it turns out many of her photos are now being praised as high art.

Maier, who was born in 1926, took pictures for most of her life, usually of people and buildings in New York City, Chicago, and Los Angeles. She also traveled to and photographed various hot spots around the world. And then she unceremoniously placed most of the rolls of film in plain cardboard boxes and stored them, undeveloped.

Fortunately, in 2007, budding filmmaker John Maloof discovered some of Maier's photos at a flea market and became intrigued by this mystery woman. He was pretty sure he'd stumbled upon a true artist but wondered, if that were the case, why she was an unknown. He posted a link to some of Maier's photos on his blog, and they went viral. He then made a documentary about her, *Finding Vivian Maier*, to try to figure out what made Maier tick and to introduce the world to her extensive portfolio.

It turns out Maier had worked for forty years as a nanny—she was even once employed by newly single dad and national talk show host Phil Donahue—and was considered a secretive, eccentric woman who shared very little about her private life and hoarded boxes and newspapers in the rooms where she lived. She took the children she cared for on outings all around Chicago, believing they should be exposed to the good, the bad, and the ugly of urban life. People said Maier was rarely without her camera, a Rolleiflex that she could hold at her waist, allowing her to take candid photographs of people without them even realizing it. Alternatively, she could entice them into having their pictures taken without the camera being a barrier between them.

Critics and professional photographers were astonished by the quality and volume of her output and how she got right up in people's faces, captured their hidden feelings, and even revealed racial inequities. In one striking photo, a black boy is shining a white boy's shoes at a shoeshine stand set up on a city street. As described by the writer Alex Kotlowitz in *Mother Jones* magazine, "Each [photo] feels like the beginning of a short story, a bit mysterious, not unlike Maier herself."

In the documentary, accomplished photographer Joel Meyerowitz says of Maier, "I wonder if she reached the end of her life and might have thought, why didn't I try to get that work out there? Some people's character prevents them from pushing that little bit you need to push to get the work seen. You know, she didn't defend herself as an artist, she just did the work."

Once Maier's oeuvre started to catch on, gallery owners around the globe began selling it. Sadly, she died before she became known and didn't achieve any artistic or financial status in her lifetime. The mystery of Maier remains unsolved. Was she, like Van Gogh with his painted portraits (as you'll see in Chapter 4, "The Sensitive Soul"), creating a connection with strangers because she felt lonely? Did she lack the confidence and contacts to get her pictures shown, particularly as a woman starting out in the 1940s and 1950s? Was the act of taking pictures satisfying enough to her that she didn't even need to see the final result? No one knows for sure.

But artist Tony Fitzpatrick believes Maier's motives *are* clear. As he told *Mother Jones*, "She made [the photographs] for all the right reasons. She made them to hold on to her place in the world. She made them because to not make them was impossible. She had no choice."

Positive Tendencies of Artisans

Following Your Bliss

Artisans are in love—with chiaroscuro, hitch kicks, dissolves, or slant rhymes. You're in love with the elements of craft, all the things, large and small, that add up to a great work of art. And all the things, large and small, that go into *producing* a great work of art.

I call this feeling joy, delight, enthrallment. Focus, dedication, immersion. If this is how doing art makes you feel, consider yourself lucky to be an Artisan!

Famous artists from every genre have described this feeling. Writer Truman Capote said, "To me, the greatest pleasure of writing is not what it's about, but the inner music that words make." Painter Claude Monet declared, "Colour is my day-long obsession, joy and torment." And composer Ludwig van Beethoven said, "Tones sound and roar and storm about me until I have set them down in notes."

Have you ever had this experience, Artisan? You're painting, painting, painting, and you look up from your canvas and realize it's dark outside, though you can't remember the sun going down. You've been working for three hours, but it felt like three minutes. Or, the phone rings and it takes you a moment to reorient yourself, to realize you're in your home "studio" (a.k.a. the corner of your bedroom) and you've typed fifteen pages but forgotten all about the conference call you're supposed to be on. Or, your kids come crashing through the front door wanting snacks and wondering what's for dinner. Dinner? Guess it's pizza tonight... again.

Psychologist Mihaly Csikszentmihalyi calls this feeling of total concentration, of complete immersion, "flow," and he explores it in depth in *Flow: The Psychology of Optimal Experience*. You may find yourself experiencing flow often or, more likely, sporadically, but if you're an Artisan, it keeps you inspired.

First flow hooks you and then it sustains you. It can also lead you to try things, creatively, you've never tried before, like techniques you'd never previously thought of or were too afraid to attempt. Csikszentmihalyi has pinpointed the precise moment at which you can achieve this state of flow: when the challenge before you is precisely at the right level for your skills. In other words, if what you're trying to do, artistically, is way beyond your natural talent level, you'll probably feel frustrated and unmotivated. If what you're doing has become rote, you'll probably feel bored. But, if you're aiming to master a new skill and it's within your reach, you just might find yourself in a state of flow. Daniel Goleman puts it this way in *The New York Times*: "A novice musician feels 'in flow' performing a well-rehearsed repertory; a master musician needs the most technically challenging pieces to get in flow; the world-class musician ups the ante by interpreting those most challenging pieces."

Stephen King, an exceedingly prolific fiction writer, knows all about flow. The current count, as of this writing, puts him at more than fifty novels (including several under a pseudonym), with reportedly 350 million copies sold and several turned into movies.

But King's life took a nearly tragic turn in 1999. He was struck by a car as he was walking along a highway in Maine. The impact caused King to be thrown into a ditch, and he suffered very serious injuries, including a collapsed right lung, multiple fractures in his right leg, a broken hip, and a scalp laceration. The bones in his leg were so shattered, doctors considered amputating but didn't ultimately need to. However, King had to have five operations in ten days and underwent a lot of physical therapy. Sitting was uncomfortable, often painful, and his stamina wasn't what it once was. Neither was his desire to write.

Fortunately, after some time had passed, King found a degree of joy in writing once again and describes it this way in his memoir *On Writing*: "On some days, that writing is a pretty grim slog. On others—more and more of them as my leg begins to heal and my mind reaccustoms itself to its old routine—I feel that buzz of happiness, that sense of having found the right words and put them in a line. It's like lifting off in an airplane; you're on the ground, on the ground, on the ground ... and then you're up, riding on a magical cushion of air and prince of all you survey. That makes me happy, because it's what I was made to do." This is one of the best descriptions of flow I've read. Here's another wonderful one, this time by Ernest Hemingway in his memoir *A Moveable Feast*. One day, during his fabled time in Paris in the 1920s with the "Lost Generation" of American expatriate writers and artists, Hemingway was sitting in a café on Place Saint-Michel in Paris, drinking a rum St. James (a common occurrence) and writing one of his stories that take place in Michigan, where he spent his teen summers. After observing a pretty woman at a table near the window, he returned to the work at hand. As he describes it, "The story was writing itself and I was having a hard time keeping up with it," and then, "I was writing it now and it was not writing itself and I did not look up nor order any more rum St. James." Hemingway was feelin' the flow.

As you've probably discovered, Artisan, being in a state of flow is an amazing high. One word of caution: be sure to appreciate flow when it occurs and not feel too discouraged when you go for a time without it. You can't force flow! But, remember, just when you think it's disappeared forever, it usually returns, giving you a boost when you need it most.

Loving the Creative Process

In Chapter 1, "The A-Lister," I raised a question posed by choreographer Twyla Tharp in her book *The Creative Habit*: "When you work, do you love the process or the result?" People with A-Lister tendencies usually pick "result" because of the enormous ego satisfaction they derive from seeing their effort amount to something tangible, something to be proud of. Also, A-Listers crave the sorts of "goodies" the finished work might bring.

Tame Your Tendencies
Reach for the Stars

As an Artisan, one of your best qualities is how much you enjoy the creative process regardless of reward. But, even if you don't have any grand expectations of serious money or recognition, it couldn't hurt to develop those ambitions a bit. So, try this: Visualize yourself opening an envelope from your agent and pulling out a check for your advance—and it has one more zero at the end than what you were expecting! Or, close your eyes and imagine the echoing sounds of clapping and feet stomping as you finish your gig in a stadium and the audience is demanding an encore. C'mon, Artisan, it has to feel a little good to you, right?

It's more common for people with Artisan tendencies, on the other hand, to pick "process" because it's the work itself, the intense dedication to improving one's technique, the pure enjoyment, that appeals the most to them.

In a long-term study of two hundred artists, Csikszentmihalyi found that a disregard early on for financial reward is a hallmark of aspiring artists who later have successful careers. He and his colleagues studied their subjects twice: first in art school and then nearly two decades later. Those who had valued the process more than the product stayed with it, and some achieved great success. But those who had been mostly motivated by fame and wealth didn't fare so well in the art world after graduation.

Your appreciation of the process may put you at a distinct advantage, Artisan. It will sustain you through the ups and downs of a creative life.

Spotlight: Painter Chuck Close

Sustained by the Creative Process

Chuck Close has suffered more tragedies and setbacks than any artist I can think of, rivaled only by fellow painter Frida Kahlo (as you'll see in Chapter 4, "The Sensitive Soul"). While Close's life circumstances might have made painting impossible for most people, it fueled his desire and even forced him to be innovative about the creative process itself. His Artisan trait of finding joy in painting galvanized him to invent new ways to keep doing it.

Close's difficulties began in childhood: he had learning disabilities, his father died when he was eleven, his mother developed breast cancer around the same time, and the family lost their home when the medical bills started piling up. He also had a condition called face blindness, where you can't recognize someone's face, sometimes even your family members, even after you just saw them a few minutes ago. Despite these extreme difficulties, he received his MFA from Yale and went on to develop his signature painting style: huge photorealistic images of... faces!

But that's not all. After an awards ceremony one night, Close didn't feel well. It turned out a blood clot had developed in his spinal column and within a matter of hours he became a quadriplegic, confined to a wheelchair. Can you imagine? This would seem to signal the end not only of life as he knew it but also of his ability to paint. But Close figured out solutions to allow him to continue doing what he loved, first holding the paintbrush in his mouth and then concocting a device to attach the brush to his hand. He paints on a huge canvas that hangs on the wall and can be rotated so he's able to reach the desired section he wants to at any given moment. He approaches the painting of a face one small square at a time, with all of the squares adding up to an original, revealing portrait.

Close has remarked that nearly everything he's done has been influenced by his learning disabilities. And, while it may seem ironic for a person with face blindness to paint faces, Close was driven to do portrait painting to commit the images of the people he loves to memory—and to prove to the art establishment that portraiture was not dead but just needed a fresh approach.

In the CBS *This Morning* series, "Note to Self," Close advises young artists to "sign on to a process and see where it takes you. You don't have to reinvent the wheel every day. Today you will do what you did yesterday and tomorrow you will do what you did today. Eventually you will get somewhere."

Keepin' It Real

One of my favorite things anyone has ever said about pretty much anything also comes from Chuck Close, who lays it out there when he admonishes artists, "Inspiration is for amateurs—the rest of us just show up and get to work." As an Artisan, you might consider this your mantra. It puts the nail in the coffin of the romanticized— and even dangerous—notion that people should wait for divine inspiration, the perfect moment, or that one, original idea before they get started on a project. The only way to get started... is to get started. (*I* said that!)

More and more famous artists in recent years have adopted the Artisan's ethos, in which a sustained effort counts for as much as, or even more than, the initial spark of creativity. Musician Jack White, of the White Stripes and Raconteurs, finds inspiration isn't always on demand when he's writing a new song. He describes it this way in the documentary *The White Stripes: Under Great White Northern Lights*: "Inspiration and work ethic—they ride right next to each other. . . . Not every day you're gonna wake up and the clouds are gonna part and rays from heaven are gonna come down and you're gonna write a song from it. Sometimes, you just get in there and just force yourself to work, and maybe something good will come out."

Writer Elizabeth Gilbert's TED talk and her book about the creative process, *Big Magic*, are, more than anything, a call to action to treat creativity as hard work and to not rely on divine intervention. She believes there might be a "cockeyed genius," as she calls it, assigned to each of us to bring forth our originality but warns it may not always be around. And, then what? As she says, "Don't be daunted. Just do your job. Continue to show up for your piece of it, whatever that might be."

I agree. There's no point in delaying and waiting for the "cockeyed genius" or muse to show up. Maybe there is no muse. Or he's hanging around with another artist for a while. Or, maybe, just maybe, the muse is within you and will reveal itself in the future. As Isabel Allende writes in her essay for the collection *Why We Write*, "Show up, show up, show up, and after a while the muse shows up, too."

Anne Lamott, the author of one of my favorite books on writing, *Bird by Bird*, has added her voice to these others, calling writing "a matter of persistence and faith and hard work" and adding, "You might as well just go ahead and get started." And more than a century earlier, composer Pyotr Ilyich Tchaikovsky wrote in a letter to his benefactress, "A self-respecting artist must not fold his hands on the pretext that he is not in the mood."

I suppose other creative types might mock you, Artisan, for your pragmatic approach to the creative process. But, you understand that it's satisfying, often frustrating, sometimes exhilarating *work*.

Nurture Your Tendencies
Set Faux Deadlines

There's nothing like external expectations to squash an Artisan's instincts to deliberate about artistic choices or, like artists of every creative type, to seek distractions. When there's a publishing deadline, commission, opening night, or scheduled studio time, all preciousness or avoidance disappears and the work ethic kicks in. You're generally good with this, Artisan. But, what happens when you aren't given a deadline by a producer or editor? You may need to establish your own self-imposed deadline and—this is important—mini-deadlines. For instance, decide for yourself that Chapter 1 is due on *x* date, Chapter 2 on *y* date, and so on, rather than feeling overwhelmed by the whole manuscript. Fool yourself into thinking your work *needs* to be completed by a particular date.

I know this can be difficult to do, but, ironically, in this case self-deception shows you're being real with yourself. Set the timer on your smartphone for the number of hours you'll devote to painting, or set a goal of the number of pages you're going to write each morning. Think of achieving these goals as requirements, not choices, and see what a difference it makes in your productivity. And consider this: maybe necessity isn't so much the mother of invention as she is a demanding, pragmatic, no-nonsense muse.

Embracing Influence, Avoiding Intimidation

If the work is what matters the most to you, not acclaim or competition, then there's no harm in acknowledging those who came before you and influenced you. It's the Artisan's way.

There is no tabula rasa. Every artist has an Etch A Sketch, one that has been scribbled on by the thousands of other artists who form their creative universe, and no matter how hard they shake it, the shadows of those other scribbles are still visible on the screen. As novelist Jeanette Winterson writes in *Art Objects*, "This is not ancestor worship, it is the lineage of art. It is not so much influence as it is connection."

My creative writing students sometimes worry that everything worth writing about has already been written or that their style is too derivative. This is a common concern for artists who fear they may be too influenced by their artistic idols. I assure my students that their approach to even well-worn themes like love or loss is uniquely theirs and that, in the beginning, writing like the authors they most admire is a time-honored tradition and will lead them to their own voice and style. The same goes for you.

As an Artisan, you understand that your artistic predecessors are part of your creative DNA and that it's fine to emulate and love your artistic "parents." You also recognize you've ultimately got to break away from these parental figures to form your own artistic identity and do your own distinctive work. That's the history of art.

In the case of writer Joan Didion, her creative parents are Ernest Hemingway and Henry James. Didion said in the *Paris Review* that reading Hemingway made her fall in love with the idea of being a writer. As a teenager, she would type out his stories to learn how sentences work, sentences she described as "smooth rivers, clear water over granite, no sinkholes."

At the same time, she drew inspiration from James, who, ironically, was the very writer Hemingway sought to write the *opposite* of. Didion described James's writing in novels such as *The Portrait of a Lady* and *The Wings of the Dove* as containing "sentences *with* sink holes," sentences "you could drown in." Read any of Didion's essays, novels, or memoirs, and you'll see hints of both authors in her work.

Author Bill Bryson credits J. D. Salinger's writing with showing him the value of choosing the right word and not settling for anything less. As Bryson recalled in a book about writing styles, *The Sound on the Page*, "I was 14, 15, reading *Catcher in the Rye* and all his other stuff. His descriptive passages—the way a person's face is reflected in the mirror or the way a tablecloth hangs, or sunlight falls—sometimes seem labored, but it doesn't matter, because at the time it was such a revelation that you could take language and use it in such a precise way."

Bryson, who is a master of humor and hyperbole, later applied this lesson to his own writing. He said, "Endlessly fussing is the only writing trick I know—never being quite satisfied.... The thing that occupies me the most is trying to get jokes right. It's so much a question of timing—the right word is so important. Only two or three times in all the years I've been writing did a joke sort of pop into my head. Most of the time you know it's there, but you've got to fuss over it endlessly." If you've read *A Walk in the Woods* or other books by Bryson, it's unlikely you would have made a connection between him and Salinger, and yet it's there in their shared obsession with wordsmithery.

It's natural for artists to be in awe of their idols—but that's different than being intimidated by them, which would be a creativity killer. Fortunately, as an Artisan, you're not easily intimidated.

Painter Henri Matisse understood the value of being open to influence. To him, along with other painters and even some writers,

painter Paul Cézanne was "the man," the artist who brought painting out of the nineteenth and into the twentieth century by representing the world in all its complexity. In his book *Matisse on Art*,
the painter wrote that he thought of Cézanne as "a sort of god of
painting." And he scoffed at those who found Cézanne's dominance
threatening, writing, "Too bad for those without the strength to
survive it. For my part, I have never avoided the influence of others."

Matisse, in turn, helped shape the next generation of mid-
twentieth-century painters. In the play *Red*, the lead character, who is
based on the abstract expressionist painter Mark Rothko, tells his assistant Ken about the impact Matisse's painting, *Red Studio*, has had
on him. Matisse's painting of his art studio broke with Western tradition by depicting the canvasses, chair, and other objects in the room
the way *he* saw them rather than using a technically accurate perspective—and all set against a nearly overwhelming tomato soup–red
background. The effect is that the objects nearly leap off the canvas.

In *Red*, Rothko says, "You could argue that everything I do
today, you can trace the bloodlines back to that painting and those
hours standing there, letting the painting work, allowing it to
move. . . . The more I looked at it the more it pulsated around me,
I was totally saturated, it swallowed me. . . . Such planes of red he
made, such energetic blocks of color, such *emotion!*" Rothko's obsessive study of Matisse's paintings led him to develop his own instantly recognizable style, which is also known for colors that seem
to pulsate with energy.

Sometimes you are so enthralled with a particular artist, but
you know you can never do what they did—it's impossible. And so
you have a choice: will you let this impossibility deter you, or will
you let it inspire you to emulate your idol, even *knowing* your goal
is unattainable?

When Jack White was eighteen, someone played him the song
"Grinnin' in Your Face" by blues singer Son House. White was a

> ### Creativity Booster
> ## Learning from Your Creative "Parents"
>
> Choose two artists in your field whose work you admire. Don't just study their techniques—copy them. Type out pages of their novels. Repeat their dance steps as precisely as you can. Do a film editing sequence exactly as they did it. And then move on. You never know what will stay with you and what will fall away, but you'll have absorbed your creative parents' excellence while carving out your own direction.

goner. As he describes it in the documentary *It Might Get Loud*, in that moment everything disappeared. There was only the singer and his song. There were no instruments being played, just Son House singing and clapping, sometimes out of rhythm. To White, "it meant everything about rock and roll, everything about expression, creativity and art. One man against the world in one song." It's still White's favorite song, and his face reflects his reverence when he plays the record. Although he knows that no matter how hard he tries, he (a white guy born in Detroit in 1975) can never be a black blues singer born in Mississippi at the start of the twentieth century, he can keep allowing the emotion, the experience, the sound to inspire him anyway.

Collaborating, or It Takes Two When It Used to Take One

Collaboration is the unsung hero of creativity. Not everyone appreciates this because it flies in the face of yet another romanticized myth about artists: they must struggle to write, compose, or sculpt in seclusion—preferably in an unheated garret in Paris. And, sure, sometimes that's the case. But, the term "solo artist" is usually a misnomer: painters and photographers often rely on models, novelists work with editors, and lyricists collaborate with composers. If you've ever collaborated with others, you probably immediately understood the benefits. Collaboration gives you the chance to bounce ideas off one another; bring strengths to offset the other's lack of knowledge or experience; boost each other's confidence; save one another from the perils of too much solitude; and, just as importantly, have fun together.

People in the performing arts are steeped in a culture of collaboration. How is it that even those with pronounced A-Lister traits form successful artistic partnerships? It's the Artisan in them that allows them to collaborate and share credit with an equally talented partner without letting ego stand in the way. Here are a couple of inspiring examples.

Rudolf Nureyev and Margot Fonteyn formed ballet's most celebrated partnership. It began at a time when many assumed Fonteyn, the grand dame of classical ballet, was set to retire. Then, in 1961, Nureyev, a ballet star in the Soviet Union at the age of twenty-two, defected at Le Bourget airport in Paris and was given political asylum in the West. During the curtain calls after their first performance together, Nureyev dropped to his knees and kissed Fonteyn's hand.

Among her many talents, Fonteyn could spin on one toe for longer than any other ballerina of her day. And Nureyev captivated audiences with his natural charisma and what's been described as his "lightning leaps" across the stage. When they danced together, the electricity between them was palpable, inspiring frenzied curtain calls and bouquet tosses onto the stage. "It is the world's most exciting dance partnership," said the choreographer Sir Frederick Ashton. "They were made to work together."

Creativity Booster
Finding a Collaborator

Artistic collaborations take many forms: cocreators, artist-muse, painter-model, songwriter-singer, composer-lyricist, director-actor, bandmates, castmates, and so on. Finding a collaborator might be as painless as walking into the room next door. That's right—scores of successful partnerships over the years have been formed between lovers, friends, or schoolmates. Here are a few questions to ask yourself when choosing an artistic partner.

- Do we have complementary talents and skills?
- Is one person more extroverted and one more introverted, making us well-suited for different tasks and roles? If not, how will we divide the responsibilities?
- Would we get on each other's nerves too much? Or develop a boss-assistant dynamic?
- Could we both/all keep our egos in check?
- Do I want to go in some new direction that only a collaborator could lead me to?
- Would collaborating instead of going it alone be just plain fun?

Fonteyn and Nureyev's on- and offstage partnership lasted fifteen years and they remained lifelong friends. In his passionate fashion, Nureyev once said, "At the end of Swan Lake, when she left the stage in her great white tutu I would have followed her to the end of the world." He also said, "We danced with one body, one soul. Margot is all I ever had, only her."

Another famous and lasting collaboration, this one in hip-hop, is between Missy Elliott and Timbaland. Elliott is the most award-winning woman in hip-hop, with multiple platinum albums and a run of hit singles that helped shape urban radio. Timbaland's distinctive production has been just as critical to the sound of hip-hop and R&B. They met in the early 1990s when they were in different bands. When Elliott decided to go solo, Timbaland produced her record *Supa Dupa Fly*, which became a massive success and featured hits such as "The Rain (Supa Dupa Fly)" and "Sock It 2 Me." Since then, the two have collaborated on some of hip-hop's most innovative hits. This is how BET described the duo: "Timbo's off-kilter rhythms and futuristic synth bleeps and Missy's outsized personality and stream-of-consciousness lyrics were the perfect package, conquering the charts and expanding the definition of what hip hop could and should be."

Cautionary Tales for the Artisan

Artisan, you need no convincing to keep writing or filming or knitting away. Now, let's look at some of the challenges you might face and tendencies you can tame so you can pursue creative endeavors while also saving space for other areas of your life.

Even Artisans Have to Eat

As an Artisan, you might find it hard sometimes to resist the romanticized image of the "starving artist," one who places art above even the most basic needs. After all, there have been so many paeans to the all-encompassing fulfillment of being an artist. The poet William Blake, for one, wrote, "I should be sorry if I had any earthly fame, for whatever natural glory a man has is so much detracted

Creativity Booster
Naming Your Fears

As an Artisan, you probably devote hours upon hours to your artistic pursuits, and that means you're putting a whole lotta eggs in one beautifully woven basket. That's always risky— even scary! The first step toward overcoming, or at least making peace with, your fears is identifying them. Some fears common to Artisans are:

- Not having enough time to devote to creativity
- Lacking the necessary funding
- Damaging relationships by prioritizing art over people
- Falling short of artistic goals
- Being "forced" to go commercial

See which of these resonate with you, and think of three more fears to add to your list. Then, answer the question "What can I do?" for each one. For instance, if your worst fear is that you'll need to go commercial to make it in the arts, write about what you could do to come to terms with this distasteful reality or how you could live reasonably well if your art doesn't sell big. Repeat this exercise with your other fears, and see if it lessens the intensity of each one.

from his spiritual glory. I wish to do nothing for profit. I wish to live for art. I want nothing whatever. I am quite happy."

The quintessential "starving artist" Vincent van Gogh echoed Blake's sentiment but with a hint of bitterness, writing to his brother, Theo: "I believe more and more that to work for the sake of the work is the principle of all great artists: not to be discouraged even though almost starving, and though one feels one has to say farewell to all material comfort."

Blake's and van Gogh's attitudes are admirable and exalted, but they don't fully acknowledge reality. The truth is, many famous artists throughout history were given the chance to pursue their passion 24/7 only because they had patrons or other financial backers. Despite Van Gogh's claims, his brother Theo sent him money on the regular, Michelangelo had Pope Julius II as a patron, and Jackson Pollock was under contract to one of New York's society's wealthy doyens in the mid-twentieth century, Peggy Guggenheim.

Artisan, do you have a wealthy and generous benefactor? If not, you're going to have to find some way to catapult yourself to instant commercial success or figure out how to preserve time for doing art while also taking care of your financial health. After all, most creatives, like other humans, have to afford rent or a mortgage, health insurance, and, of course, gallons of overpriced coffee. "Following your bliss" doesn't have to mean following it into bankruptcy, defaults on your student loans, or foreclosure on your home.

And, so, I have a suggestion (trigger warning: this might distress Artisans and non-Artisans alike who were not expecting to see the J-word in a creativity book). Yep, you might have to get a job.

For some Artisans, this can understandably come as unwelcome news. After all, you've discovered what you're great at, and you're more than willing to devote those 10,000 hours to mastering it. Unfortunately, receiving a fair wage for art is not a given, and so you may have to pursue other means of compensation.

In *Real Artists Have Day Jobs*, Sara Benincasa does a takedown of the attitude that aspiring artists must devote themselves full time to their creative pursuits or they're somehow poseurs. She writes, "Art does not need your full-time attention. Art does not demand that you starve in order to afford paint and canvas and brushes, or knitting needles and yarn, or a chainsaw for your badass ice sculptures, or whatever your tools may be for your particular medium."

Benincasa also writes, "Real artists have day jobs, and night jobs, and afternoon jobs. Real artists make things other than art, and then they make time to make art because art is screaming to get out from inside them." She also points out a truism worth noting: most famous artists held down a nine-to-five job before becoming known. John Green was a chaplain at a children's hospital and intended to attend seminary and become an Episcopal priest. Instead, he wound up using his experiences working with young, terminally ill patients as the basis for his beloved novel *The Fault in Our Stars*. For seven years, author Haruki Murakami and his wife were the proprietors of a Tokyo coffeehouse and jazz bar named for one of their pets, Peter Cat (which later become the name of a character in Murakami's novel *South of the Border, West of the Sun*).

Writer and humorist David Sedaris was discovered when public radio host Ira Glass heard him doing a reading of his diary. Glass then invited him to read his essays on NPR, and this launched an amazing literary career. But did you know that even after Sedaris began attracting a following, he continued with his day job, cleaning houses? In a *Fresh Air* radio interview, host Terry Gross asked Sedaris if it bothered him that he'd had to continue cleaning houses for a while instead of devoting all his time to writing. Sedaris answered, "I like to think that all work is pretty much equal" and described the satisfaction in doing a job where there is "a before and an after." When Gross pressed him about how splitting his time affected his identity as a writer, he responded that he supposed he could do nothing all day and write at night for the sake of calling himself a writer, but that seemed foolish to him. Point well taken, Sedaris.

Some famous artists have continued in their day jobs for decades while creating magnificent art: writer-artist Henry Darger was a custodian, comic book writer Harvey Pekar was a Veterans Administration hospital clerk, and poet William Carlos Williams was a doctor. Another doctor, Abraham Verghese, made the unusual move of temporarily leaving medicine to get his MFA from the Iowa Writers' Workshop and start writing fiction. He then returned to the medical field, and as of this writing serves as a tenured professor at Stanford Medical School. His well-received 2009 novel, *Cutting for Stone*, an elegy for a lost way of life in Ethiopia, confirmed his decision to have a dual-track career.

You, too, must find various strategies over the course of a lifetime to pursue creativity while also earning a living—Artisans always have, and they always will. See the Sidebar for some specific suggestions.

The Friends & Family Plan

If you're being honest with yourself, Artisan, you might have to admit that working 'round the clock on creative projects is what you most want to do in the world. That will make you a prolific artist, but it's almost guaranteed to hurt some of your relationships.

As the biographer Matthew J. Bruccoli observes in *Fitzgerald and Hemingway: A Dangerous Friendship*, "Writers tend to be bad risks as friends—probably for much the same reasons that they are bad matrimonial risks. They expend the best part of themselves in their work." Certainly, some writers, and artists more generally, are wonderful friends and romantic partners—you might even know of some. You might even be one!

But, when it comes to Artisans, "work-life balance" is often not in their lexicon. In fact, a 2016 study in the *Academy of*

Tame Your Tendencies
Go for the Dough

As an Artisan, you might dream of a life devoted to art, without any money concerns, but sometimes reality bites—and it could bite you. It's possible you'll be one of the lucky ones who can immediately earn a living at art. If not, here are some other approaches to consider: Pursue a career path related to your creative interests (in publishing if you're a writer, or with a code academy if you're an app creator), and use the nights or wee hours of the morning on artistic projects. If you're still young, try to get a job with predictable or limited hours and live with roommates and eat ramen for a couple of years after you graduate from high school or college until you see if your artistic ambitions pay off. Apply for grants or fellowships or launch a Kickstarter campaign that will help support you as you produce your novel, art exhibition, or record. Write for publications offering fair compensation instead of giving away your words and thoughts for free. These strategies may not be feasible for everyone depending on current life circumstances, but they just might work for you.

Management Journal found that people who get to be especially creative at an office job spend less time with their spouses at home, and the time they do spend is of lower quality. By extension, the same finding might apply to Artisans.

Can Artisans put family first? Or, does the very nature of their work require such sharpened focus as to make this impossible? And why, if other people struggle and often fail to achieve work-family balance, would we expect Artisans, with their devotion to art, to succeed?

This issue came up during an inspirational *Inside the Actors Studio* episode with director Francis Ford Coppola. Coppola gently admonished the students in the audience not to delay starting a family until they're established, saying he found that having a family as a young man and needing to financially support it was not an obstacle to making movies but, instead, served as the impetus. And yet I believe he romanticized the family-art connection rather than acknowledging that conflicts can arise when a celebrated artist is also a spouse and parent.

Coppola's wife, Eleanor, brought a very different perspective in her 2008 memoir, *Notes on a Life: A Portrait of a Marriage*. Eleanor quotes singer Tom Waits as saying, "'Family and career don't like each other . . . one is always trying to eat the other.'" Case in point: Coppola's notorious three-year obsessive devotion to the making of *Apocalypse Now* in the Philippines, an experience that nearly destroyed him and almost killed actor Martin Sheen, who suffered a heart attack during the making of the movie.

Eleanor captures the harrowing experience in her award-winning documentary *Heart of Darkness: A Filmmaker's Apocalypse*. In an interview with CNN, she says, "When you do something that's the most extreme and hardest thing you have ever done—everything is in jeopardy; your personal life, your financial life is in jeopardy and people's lives were literally in jeopardy."

True, Coppola's reputation as a devoted family man remains intact, in no small part because he often involves his family, including daughter-turned-director Sofia Coppola, in his film productions. Nevertheless, if you're someone who values your family and friends, it's worth considering what you can do to make them feel as important to you as your art is.

The Takeaway

If you're an Artisan or someone with Artisan tendencies, creativity feeds you, it absorbs you, and it might even have too great a hold on you at times. What can you do to make the most of your dedication to art while also making sure you look up from the laptop or canvas every now and then?

- Indulge your inner nerd; it's essential to your artistry.
- Enjoy the highs of creativity, but don't become dependent on them. They can be addictive, like a drug.
- Being an art purist is admirable, but don't forget you've also got to make a living.
- Be open to a whole world of influences and then develop your own distinct voice and point of view.
- Promote yourself—your work deserves to be seen by multitudes.
- Don't forget your friends and family—man or woman cannot live for art alone.

Chapter 3

THE GAME CHANGER: CREATING SOMETHING ENTIRELY NEW

ᴖᴗᴖ

Do not go where the path may lead. Go instead
where there is no path and leave a trail.

—RALPH WALDO EMERSON, "SELF-RELIANCE"

Were you one of those kids who refused to color within the lines?
Why would you, when you could draw your own pictures? (Yours
were way cooler than the ones in the coloring book your mom gave
you.)

When you were assigned yet another five-paragraph essay for
tenth-grade English, did you hand in a short story instead? One
your teacher secretly loved but had to give you an "F" for? You
didn't care—you even bragged about it to your friends.

Maybe you're trying to get funding for a film no one seems to
"get." But you're certain they will someday.

You just might be a Game Changer.

Why Do Game Changers Create?

If you're a Game Changer or you have Game Changer tendencies, you want to make new, revolutionary, visionary art. You have the devotion of the Artisan and the ego of the A-Lister, and that's an unbeatable combo. Here are some reasons why you create.

Because you love what you do *and* you have a ton of ideas—or one outstanding idea (if you say so yourself, and you do). Because you can't do same-old-same-old—it's not in your nature. Because your top-ten list of creators is composed of people who were treated like outcasts for most of their lives but were ultimately hailed as geniuses. Because you're inspired by a mentor and also inspired to outdo him or her someday. Because nothing would bring you more pleasure than to shake things up in the stuffy, predictable, corporatized, vanilla world of visual art/music/publishing/graphic design.

Snapshot of a Game Changer

Game Changers believe what they're doing is wholly original, surpasses what's been done before, and may even mark the beginnings of a new genre.

Write another traditional sonnet? If it can't be better than Shakespeare's, why do it? As a Game Changer, you'd rather be an original, if unknown, writer than a second-rate Shakespeare (even if being a second-rate Shakespeare would still make you one of the most recognized poets in the world). Though, truly, anonymity is not your preference.

Game Changers aren't looking to change the world, politically—that's what motivates Activists. Instead, they're aiming to expand the limits of art and, in turn, get people to see the world differently.

Artistic Personality Quiz
So, You Think You're a Game Changer

1. When others question whether something new in art can really be done, do you respond with "Why not"?
2. Are you driven to rebel against the status quo in art and stake out new territory?
3. Are you hoping to set the music or publishing or theater world on fire?
4. Do you want to save art from the commercial interests threatening to ruin it?
5. Do you sometimes feel like other people don't "get" what you're doing, artistically?
6. Are you opposed to labeling and categorizing art and excited to do genre-defying projects?
7. Are you involved in a prominent art scene or serving as the leader of a movement (maybe even one with a manifesto)?
8. Have you purposely escaped the influence of your artistic idols?
9. Can you force yourself to wait for others to catch on to your vision, even if it takes years or decades?
10. Do you have the fortitude to stay the course even if you're the target of criticism?

If you answered "yes" to most of these questions, you are a Game Changer. And, if you answered "yes" to even a few of these questions, you have some strong Game Changer tendencies. Either way, read on.

Game Changers often become restless and bored with following the conventions of, let's say, figure painting and, as a result, experiment with new approaches that renew their excitement for their craft.

Wherever there's a new art movement or manifesto, you can be sure the founders or authors were Game Changers. But, that's not to say their goals stem solely from an adolescent rebellion against tradition. Game Changers, like other creative people, are ultimately *acting*, not just *reacting*. If you identify with this type, you're busy discovering your own voice and style, being inventive and original, making your mark, making history, or rescuing art from the soulless moguls and artists who are "ruining" it.

Do Game Changers sometimes fall into the trap that new is better simply because it hasn't been done before? Yes. And Game Changers can feel embittered when no one follows them into virgin territory.

But, fear not, Game Changer—your belief in yourself and your faith in the limitless possibilities of art will keep you steadfast in your pursuit of inventive, daring work.

Varieties of Game Changers

You might be the sort of Game Changer who wants to shock and awe an audience with your bold, even "offensive," art. Or, you might be the kind of Game Changer who wants to start a movement, pen a manifesto, or drive your car over establishment art and then put the car in reverse and crush it again for good measure.

See the Sidebar for a list of varieties of Game Changers, and read on for an exploration of some of the most common ones.

The Visionary

George Bernard Shaw captured the can-do attitude of Game Changers when he wrote these lines for his play *Back to Methuselah*:

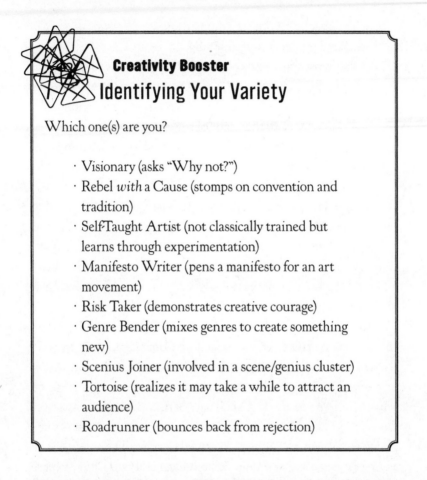

Creativity Booster

Identifying Your Variety

Which one(s) are you?

- Visionary (asks "Why not?")
- Rebel *with* a Cause (stomps on convention and tradition)
- Self-Taught Artist (not classically trained but learns through experimentation)
- Manifesto Writer (pens a manifesto for an art movement)
- Risk Taker (demonstrates creative courage)
- Genre Bender (mixes genres to create something new)
- Scenius Joiner (involved in a scene/genius cluster)
- Tortoise (realizes it may take a while to attract an audience)
- Roadrunner (bounces back from rejection)

"You see things; and you say, 'Why?' But I dream things that never were; and I say, 'Why not?'"

Asking "why not" is a defining characteristic of Game Changers, and it's powered some of the greatest breakthroughs in art history.

Game Changers are not just changing art, they're expanding conceptions of what's possible. In some cases, they—and possibly you—are what Sigmund Freud's disciple Carl Jung called the creators of "visionary art," which Jung defines this way:

- It connects us with superhuman and timeless worlds beyond our conscious knowing.
- The artist transcends personal fate and begins to speak to and for humankind.
- The "answer" is channeled through receptive individuals in response to the needs of the entire race.
- The artist captures and expresses the spiritual meaning of the culture.

In modern terms, I think the visionary artist is that once-in-a-generation figure—often a singer—who captures something that's simmering in a culture's cauldron, forcing it to bubble to the surface. When I ask my students who they'd call a visionary artist, they usually mention Bob Dylan, John Lennon, or Beyoncé. Who would you name?

Author John Lobell writes in his book *Visionary Creativity* that visionary artists, whom I'm calling Game Changers, "respond to the culture of their day, and at the same time, they advance it into an emerging world, creating for us an entirely new stage on which we live our lives." Lobell says artists throughout the ages foresaw a new world on the horizon and were amazed others were oblivious to changes that were destined to come. They were driven to do original art that would make the general population experience what they experienced, see what they saw.

In other words, Game Changer, you are someone who is both of your culture and ahead of it, someone who lives with one foot in the present and one in the future. The challenges are: Can you either drag others along or shove them forward? And are you willing to withstand resistance or ridicule if your vision is rejected at first?

You'll need to develop the faith in yourself and imperviousness to criticism embodied by the fictional architect Howard Roark in Ayn Rand's novel *The Fountainhead*. No one represents the Game

Changer credo better. Nearly every speech of his (and there are many) illuminates the guiding philosophy of Game Changers. In one passage he says, "Throughout the centuries there were men who took first steps down new roads armed with nothing but their own vision. Their goals differed, but they all had this in common: that the step was first, the road new, the vision unborrowed, and the response they received—hatred. The great creators—the thinkers, the artists, the scientists, the inventors—stood alone against the people of their time. Every great new thought was opposed. Every great new invention was denounced." And yet, history's innovators ultimately won.

You'll notice that, unlike Artisans, the most extreme Game Changers do not tend to credit, or even recognize, those who preceded them and influenced them. This, too, is a sentiment Roark espouses, saying, "I set my own standards. I inherit nothing. I stand at the end of no tradition. I may, perhaps, stand at the beginning of one."

📷 Spotlight: Performance Artist Marina Abramović

Imaginative, Confident, Determined

In 2010, for a period of eleven weeks, there was a woman who proved her Game Changer bona fides day after day. Dressed head-to-toe in a monochromatic red, black, or white gown and possessing superhuman powers of concentration and endurance, she sat on a chair placed in the center of a large white room at the Museum of Modern Art (MoMA) in New York City for hours upon hours (totaling more than seven hundred), staring into the eyes of one audience participant after another after another as they occupied the seat opposite her. In total, 15,000 people—mostly strangers, a few friends or exes—sat with her, and 750,000 visited the exhibition. Many stood in line for hours. Some who sat smiled; some were moved to tears. Some found the experience so moving, they returned multiple times.

The woman in the center of the room—and the center of the controversy about the "legitimacy" of performance art for decades—was Serbian-born artist **Marina Abramović**. What gave her the certainty that staring into the eyes of another person constitutes art?

She appears to have an unshakable faith in her artistry, along with a passion for it and decades of experience defending it. Here are two of her earlier game-changing performances: in Serbia in 1974, she placed seventy-two items, including a feather boa, roses, and—to up the ante—a loaded pistol on a table and invited members of the public to use them on her. *Spoiler alert*: she survived. A year later, in an attempt to push her physical body to its limits, she consumed over two pounds of honey, drank a bottle of wine and then broke the bottle with her hands, and carved a five-pointed Communist star into her abdomen with a razor blade.

Prior to the MoMA exhibit, Abramović said she wanted to bring back the pureness of art, which she believes is all about energy. In the film of the event and the preparation leading up to it, *Marina Abramović: The Artist Is Present*, she elaborates on this idea, saying, "The hardest thing is to do actually something which is close to nothing.... There's just you: pure presence. You have to rely on yourself, nothing else."

If you tend toward a healthy skepticism, you might be rolling your eyes or muttering "give me a break" just about now. Even if you're a Game Changer, you have your limits! And, if you heard about the event at the time or remember the live audience and celebrities, including James Franco and Sharon Stone, plus cameras in the room feeding the media frenzy, or even Jay Z's adaptation of the performance, you might be forgiven for questioning whether it was art or hype.

But if you were there or have seen the footage, I think you'd probably agree it was, indeed, art. The performance was mesmerizing and even full of pathos. Abramović was once part of a romantic and artistic duo with another performance artist, Ulay. After years of estrangement, he came to her performance, and when he sat opposite her and she opened her eyes and saw him, it was a supremely touching moment.

You might also be surprised by the degree of thought, planning, and training that such a performance requires. You think it's easy to sit still and go without food or even a visit to the bathroom for hours on end? (Abramović does, however, figure out a clever way to pee without ever getting up from her chair. TMI?) Think back on all those late-night college discussions in which someone asked, "What is art?" and you might find your answer in Abramović's performance piece.

Rebel with a Cause

In an episode of the sixth season of *Sex and the City*, Carrie worries her new boyfriend, Berger (who later breaks up with her by Post-It note—yeah, *that* guy), is not over his ex. He still uses a sleep machine at night that she gave him, set to frog sounds, and it drives Carrie crazy. After Berger finally admits the ex broke his heart, Carrie gives him a new sleep machine for a new start—and guess which sound it doesn't include? If you guessed *ribbit*, you'd be right.

Sometimes art is like that. The new is created, in part, in reaction to the old. Impressionism took a stand against the art academy and its restrictive views as to which subjects are paint-worthy. Modern dance fought against the constraints of classical ballet. Punk was a critique of corporate stadium rock. If you think about your favorite type of art in any creative field, you can trace its beginnings to a marked departure from what came before.

Yet, these movements were not just a reaction to the past. They were about artists discovering their own voices and styles, being inventive and original, "rescuing" art from those who'd sullied it, and pioneering artwork powerful enough to dethrone, or at least destabilize, the old.

While this may sound lofty, it's important to also acknowledge that sometimes the decision to break with tradition is more personal (and even vindictive) than you might expect, especially if that tradition breaker is Ernest Hemingway.

Hemingway didn't simply stumble upon his distinctive, never-before-seen style of writing; he had a *goal*. He wanted to communicate action and emotion with the simplest, most direct, most succinct style—a style of writing commonly found in newspapers (not novels) at the time. He wanted to write in a fashion that was the opposite of what he considered the flowery, overwrought manner respected in the early twentieth century, particularly in the novels of Henry James. There's a special reason for this.

The first Mrs. Hemingway, Hadley, once told a newspaper reporter who was writing a profile of Hemingway that her favorite author was Henry James (ouch). Years later she confided in a friend that her husband had "exploded" over her remark and that "James was a scurrilous word in our household." No surprise there!

It can be hard to appreciate what a radical departure Hemingway's writing was because his novels and stories have been read and studied for decades, and his style has been emulated and imitated by so many writers since. But, radical it was.

Hemingway describes his technique in *A Moveable Feast*, a memoir written in the early 1960s looking back on his years as a fiction writer in Paris in the 1920s, like this: "Since I had started to break down all my writing and get rid of all facility and try to make instead of describe, writing had been wonderful to do. But it was very difficult."

His advice to himself and aspiring authors, advice that has equally inspired and intimidated generations of writers since, is this: "All you have to do is write one true sentence. Write the truest sentence that you know." For Game Changers, even better if that true sentence is noticeably different from the style du jour.

When you are working on a creative project, do you find yourself wondering, what's an original way of approaching this? Why do so many rock songs/short stories/documentary films follow the same, tired structure, and what if I wrote one with an unexpected, surprising, maybe even jarring structure instead? That's a good indication that you're a Game Changer.

The Self-Taught Artist

Creativity does not begin or end with expertise, especially for a Game Changer. It's true (as I discuss in Chapter 2, "The Artisan") that practice is a key factor in achieving mastery. But, extreme practice also has a potential downside.

Psychologist Scott Barry Kaufman claims in *Scientific American* that deliberate practice can be antithetical to those who strive for originality (that's you, Game Changer). As Kaufman writes, "Expertise acquisition appears to be the least interesting aspect of creativity as creators tend to be in a hurry to learn what exists so that they can go beyond what exists." He further says that "too much knowledge can impair flexibility" and points to research showing that in some fields, such as creative writing, there is an optimal amount of formal schooling, after which the likelihood of a student producing original work decreases. Even as a creative writing teacher, I can see how that might be the case for some, though not all, students.

When it comes to pop music, none of the Beatles had formal training—they couldn't even read musical notations—and yet think of what they accomplished! Their producer, George Martin,

a trained classical musician, believed John Lennon's and Paul Mc-
Cartney's ignorance of the rules was key to their songwriting. In
the book *A Day in the Life*, he's quoted as saying, "Once you start
being taught things, your mind is channeled in a particular way.
Paul didn't have that channeling, so he had freedom, and could
think of things that I would have considered outrageous. I could
admire them, but my musical training would have prevented me
from thinking of them myself."

While Martin was being humble, it's worth noting that he also
described himself as the "realizer" of the Beatles' musical ideas, especially on the *Sgt. Pepper* album, where they relied on him to orches-
trate classical bits and incorporate sound effects that they, on their
own, weren't capable of doing. Think of the thrilling crescendo on
"A Day in the Life," for instance. It was the Beatles' experimentation combined with Martin's musical training that produced the
winning formula.

And so, Game Changer, I believe the lesson to learn is this: experiment, get educated, and then let that education inform—but
not hamper—your vision and originality.

Manifesto Writer

It's a sure sign you're a Game Changer if you're the leader of a movement and you pen its manifesto. Manifestos were de rigueur in
modernist, avant-garde movements of the early twentieth century,
fell out of favor, and then became popular again in the 1990s with
the advent of the Internet. They're usually written against tradition and in favor of change, and their rhetoric is often inflammatory
and, better yet, amusing.

Here are three art movements with especially memorable
manifestos:

Futurism was founded in Italy in 1909 and issued the first art manifesto of the twentieth century, written by philosopher and writer Filippo Tommaso Marinetti. It was even published on the front page of the French newspaper *Le Figaro*. Can you imagine an art manifesto appearing on the front page of any newspaper today? It starts off with these three declarations:

1. We intend to sing the love of danger, the habit of energy and fearlessness.
2. Courage, boldness, and rebellion will be the essential elements in our poetry.
3. Up to now, literature has extolled a contemplative stillness, rapture and reverie. We intend to glorify aggressive action, a restive wakefulness, life at the double, the slap and the punching fist.

That last part is, obviously, the best.

Dadaism was founded in Zurich in 1916 by Tristan Tzara, a Romanian and French poet and essayist. Dadaists believed nationalism and rationalism caused World War I, and art in all genres should work against these beliefs. The founding manifesto includes these declarative lines: "Dada was born of a need for independence, of a distrust toward unity. Those who are with us preserve their freedom. We recognize no theory."

Stuckism is a British art movement founded in 1999, with the Stuckists proclaiming they were "against conceptualism, hedonism, and the cult of the ego-artist." Every year, the Stuckists famously demonstrate outside the Tate Museum in London, where the Turner Prize, named after the English painter J. M. W. Turner, is presented to a visual artist under age fifty. Here are some of their key points, presented as a syllogism of sorts:

- Painting is the medium of self-discovery.
- Artists who don't paint aren't artists.
- Art that has to be in a gallery to be art isn't art.

It's hard to argue with Stuckists unless, of course, you're an artist who doesn't paint, which would account for the majority of artists today.

You may not be a member of an official movement, but that doesn't have to keep you from penning an individual manifesto. Silly as that may seem, it could actually help you clarify your personal goals for doing boundary-breaking art.

Positive Tendencies of Game Changers

Possessing Creative Courage

Psychologist Rollo May described artists with the Game Changer artistic personality as having "creative courage." This is how he explained the term in *The Courage to Create*: "Whereas moral courage is the righting of wrongs, creative courage, in contrast, is the discovering of new forms, new symbols, new patterns on which a new society can be built."

While May's definition of creative courage may sound pretty pie in the sky, you can bring it down to earth by applying it to your own real-life situation. Say you brought a personal essay into your writing workshop and no one "got" why you were using second person instead of first, which would be the obvious choice in this genre. You listened to what others had to say, but if your teacher's or your classmates' objection was "It's just not done that way" or "Personal essay *has* to be written in first person," you didn't automatically cave in to their demands. You considered their criticism but didn't change the point of view just because of tradition. You defended your artistic decision. That's an example of creative courage, even on a small scale.

Someday, Game Changer, you might become an artist who demonstrates such courage on a grand scale. You're on track to join the ranks of artists, like these, who've made creative courage their defining trait.

Édouard Manet, the founder of the French Impressionist movement of the late nineteenth century, was one of the first artists to paint modern life and "regular folk" rather than the traditional subjects of European oil painting. His risqué scenes, in particular, shocked and offended French society. In *Le Déjeuner sur l'Herbe*, for instance, a nude female is lunching with two fully clothed men; she gazes straight ahead while the men interact only with each other and a half-dressed woman behind them bathes in a stream. While Manet's depiction may not be a feminist's dream, he achieved his aims of shaking up the staid art world by refusing to be circumscribed by "approved" subjects for painting. One interpretation of the work is that it shows the rampant prostitution in the Bois de Boulogne, a large park at the western outskirts of Paris. While the presence of prostitutes there was common knowledge, it was considered an unsuitable subject for a painting.

Déjeuner was also both a tribute to and a departure from Renaissance works held in deep reverence at the time. According to the writer Marcel Proust, one day when he and Manet were lounging together by the Seine, Manet told him he was working on a painting that would present a modern approach to famous works by the painter Giorgione but with "people like those we see over there."

Not surprisingly, *Le Déjeuner sur l'Herbe* was rejected by the official Salon of 1863, and so Manet exhibited it and two other paintings in the upstart Salon des Refuses, where it caused a stir. Its impact on other artists cannot be overstated: over the years it inspired painters Claude Monet, Paul Cézanne, Pablo Picasso, and Paul Gauguin, along with the writer Émile Zola and the filmmaker Jean Renoir.

Frank Lloyd Wright was one of the world's preeminent architects (he called himself "the greatest living architect"). He lived to age ninety-one and worked right up to the time of his death, dominating much of the field throughout the twentieth century and beyond. In typical Game Changer fashion, he was both the bad boy of American architecture and the leader of a thriving modern movement.

When Wright first appeared, American architecture was still dominated by European styles dating back centuries. Wright's inspiration, instead, was the broad expanses of the prairie landscape where he grew up. He pioneered the Prairie School movement, in which form follows function and buildings are designed in harmony with their environment. Among his most famous structures is Fallingwater, a house built over a waterfall in rural southwestern Pennsylvania and considered the best all-time work of American architecture by the American Institute of Architects.

Wright was also a critic of the city skyscraper, pleading for an end to America's "lust for ugliness" and declaring that a boxlike building is "more of a coffin for the human spirit than an inspiration." When he received the commission for the Guggenheim Museum in New York City in 1943, he designed it in direct opposition to the skyscrapers that defined the city's famous skyline. Much to the chagrin of the artists who worried their work would never hang correctly, Wright designed the Guggenheim in a cylindrical shape, with a single gallery running along a ramp coiling up from the ground. His inventive style caused a hubbub (one critic called it "an indigestible hot cross bun"), but the Guggenheim became revered as a New York City landmark. Sadly, Wright died before the project was completed.

Jack Kerouac was a pioneer of the Beat Generation and helped define the movement with his groundbreaking novel *On the Road*, a favorite to this day of hipsters and their formerly hippie parents. The book was written on a single 120-foot roll of paper, which his editor didn't appreciate, and so their relationship ended. It took seven years for the book to be published, but when it came out in 1957, it became the bible of the counterculture and influenced decades of writers enamored with Kerouac's cool and his stream-of-consciousness style.

Alfred Hitchcock is called "The Master" for many reasons, from his understanding of the audience's collective psyche to his genius at generating suspense to his invention of special effects too numerous to list.

What's less known is that he also changed how people watch movies. When *Psycho* was released in 1960, he put armed guards in the theaters so audience members couldn't enter during the last twenty minutes. Before *Psycho*, believe it or not, people would go to the cinema and start watching the movie from wherever it was in the run time and then wait until after the film ended, the B film ended, the cartoons played, and the film started over in order to see what they'd missed. After *Psycho*, moviegoers began coming to the theater at a scheduled time so they could watch the film from beginning to end. As a result, Hitchcock also changed how movies were written because screenwriters could now write for an audience that was expected to see the movie from start to finish, rather than be forced to articulate in each scene who the hero is, who the villain is, and so on.

A known admirer of Hitchcock, Jean-Luc Godard was one of the defining filmmakers of the French New Wave movement. While he was accused of being "anti-Hollywood," the opposite was also true. He loved Hollywood movies, especially noir, and he wanted to both honor and break with tradition. He would use a stock noir plot and then include actions and techniques normally not shown in movies. In 1960's *Breathless*, while the film focuses on the relationship between the French main character, Michel, who kills a cop, and his American girlfriend, Patricia, most of the action revolves around the couple lying in bed, talking about things unrelated to the plot or Michel's crime.

Here's another twist on convention: while traditional Hollywood filmmakers tried to make editing fluid and, therefore, unnoticeable, Godard used techniques to expose the "invisible hand" of the Hollywood editing system. For instance, in *Masculin Feminin*, Godard used jump cuts, two shots in juxtaposition where the camera angle slightly changes and produces a jarring effect. Also, in *Pierrot le Fou*, the main character looks into the camera and addresses the audience, breaking the fourth wall. Filmmakers have been copying these techniques ever since, further cementing Godard's reputation as a Game Changer.

One of chef and author Julia Child's greatest achievements was popularizing French cuisine in the United States. After living in France for a few years and becoming an expert in cooking the French way, she was inspired to cowrite the two-volume, three-pound cookbook *Mastering the Art of French Cooking*, with Volume 1 published in 1961 and Volume 2 in 1970. To promote the books, she made an omelet on Boston's public television station, demonstrating how the average home cook could master the basics of French cuisine. To an American homemaker, whose cooking was limited to staples like hamburgers, steak, and spaghetti and meatballs, making a dish like coq au vin was intimidating until Julia, with her easygoing manner and humor, made it seem doable. She became the first woman inducted into the Culinary Institute of America's Hall of Fame and was awarded France's highest honor, the Légion d'Honneur.

The Sugarhill Gang recorded "Rapper's Delight" in a single take and released it in 1979. While it wasn't the first rap song, it took the art form from clubs to a commercial level when the twelve-inch format was released. Even though the song was fifteen minutes long, urban radio played it. Next, the Sugarhill Gang recorded a seven-minute version for pop stations and introduced the black neighborhood sound to a white audience. Harry Allen, from *The Village Voice* and *Vibe* magazine, wrote that "what hip-hop fashioned was a conduit whereby people who normally are locked out of telling get to tell."

In 2012, the Library of Congress preserved "Rapper's Delight" in the National Recording Registry along with other songs the institution considered "culturally, historically, or aesthetically significant." "Rapper's Delight" has also made numerous lists of the best or most influential songs.

Lin-Manuel Miranda, a librettist, rapper, composer, and actor, is best known for the Broadway musicals *In the Heights* and the smash hit *Hamilton*. (You know you've made it when your musical is parodied on television shows, as *Hamilton*, with a guest appearance by Miranda, was on *Inside Amy Schumer*.) While *Hamilton* tells the story of the white Founding Fathers, it defies expectations by featuring a diverse cast and modern rhythms, including hip-hop. It also highlights the role of immigrants as crucial to the success of the nation, a polarizing issue in current times. At the Seventieth Annual Tonys in 2016, *Hamilton* won eleven awards, including Best Musical. Better yet, the year before, Miranda got to perform a freestyle rap for President Obama in the White House Rose Garden.

Defying Genre, or Genre Is Over! (If You Want It)

Genre bending is the province of Game Changers. You figure, why does the border separating this genre from that one have to be so rigid, so impermeable? What if I do a mash-up of sorts to produce an original piece? Your refusal to be confined by categories and labels and your willingness to experiment positions you to produce game-changing art. Take these examples: Truman Capote brought fiction to journalism. Bob Dylan and Paul Simon brought poetry to rock. Patti Smith brought rock to poetry. Sylvia Plath brought poetry to fiction. Jean Toomer's book *Cane* defied the limitations of any one genre. Each of these writers made a conscious choice to cross genres—it was not just a happy accident.

In her memoir *Just Kids*, Smith, a.k.a. the Queen of Punk, writes, "I wanted to infuse the written word with the immediacy and frontal attack of rock and roll." I got to see Smith in conversation with *The New Yorker* editor David Remnick at the 2015 New Yorker Festival. It was followed by a surprise performance of "Because the Night," where Remnick admirably accompanied Smith on guitar. There, she reiterated what had motivated her as a poet, saying, "I just wanted to make poetry a little more visceral." As she progressed from poet to songwriter, that's exactly what she did.

As evidence of writer Sylvia Plath's genre-bending Game Changer tendencies, when she started conceiving plans for her novel *The Bell Jar*, she described a *Eureka* moment, writing in her journal, "Use words as a poet uses words. *That* is it!" She continued with, "I must be a word-artist." A "word-artist" was not only a new type of writer, it was a new sense of self for Plath—her artistic identity. Arriving at this identity and sense of purpose helped inspire her to bring her poetic sensibilities to her prose writing in a way she might never have otherwise.

The biracial Harlem Renaissance writer Jean Toomer was not going to feel constrained by traditional notions of genre—not when he even defied traditional definitions of race, sometimes allowing himself to be considered black while other times "passing" as white.

Creativity Booster
Trying Some Genre Bending

Like most creative people, even Game Changers can find themselves staying too ensconced in their comfort zone. Try doing a little genre-bending, and see what you come up with. It might be a disastrous mess, but, then again, it might be fantastic. If you write rock songs, see what happens if you try a hip-hop beat. If you paint watercolors, maybe add in pen and ink. If you write fiction, you could incorporate the characters' letters or diary entries. Mix it up—you might be pleasantly surprised at the results.

Cane is a series of vignettes about the origins and experiences of several black characters in the American South. In his autobiography, Toomer described the book as a "swan-song" for the end of an era, the end of what he called the folk spirit. The vignettes alternate in structure between narrative prose, poetry, and play-like passages of dialogue. As a result, *Cane* defies classification.

Each of these writers was willing to be laughed at or scorned. They knew they might not be favorably reviewed by critics or well received by the public. But they forged ahead anyway, doing their own work in their own inimitable style.

Joining a Scenius

Despite a Game Changer's proclivity toward independence, now and then he or she will join a "genius cluster" of visionary artists in a city considered the epicenter of culture in its time. In describing this phenomenon, musician and producer Brian Eno coined the term "scenius," introducing it into the lexicon at the 2009 Luminous Festival.

When Eno was an art student, he, like most of us, learned that there were a few great figures throughout Western history who magically appeared and single-handedly sparked an art revolution. But that didn't make sense to Eno. Instead, he realized that now and then there were "very fertile scenes involving lots and lots of people—some of them artists, some of them collectors, some of them curators, thinkers, theorists, people who were fashionable and knew what the hip things were—all sorts of people who created a kind of ecology of talent. And out of that ecology arose some wonderful work." Thus, scene + genius = scenius.

Have you ever wondered how geniuses like Leonardo da Vinci and Michelangelo happened to be in Florence, Italy, at the same time? Not to mention a cadre of other well-known painters and sculptors? In his book *The Geography of Genius*, Eric Weiner notes two qualities that go into the making of a scenius and points to Florence during the Renaissance as an example of both: (1) an openness to innovation, and (2) an equal openness to talented outsiders. As Weiner said in an interview on *PBS NewsHour*, "People were living out of each other's intellectual pockets. They were sharing ideas. There was enough trust to share your ideas, but enough tension to create some sparks."

He also pointed to Vienna in the late eighteenth century, where Beethoven, Mozart, and Haydn all made their mark. Yet none of them had been raised there; they were all immigrants. Vienna's spirit of innovation attracted these and other artists to the city, and once they moved there, they helped turn the city into a cultural hotbed.

Today, a scenius for writers has taken root in Brooklyn, for musicians in Philly, and for filmmakers in Austin. If you're a Game

Changer, the energy of a scenius can infuse you with excitement and inspire you to join in the artistic conversation swirling around you at coffee shops, in bookstores, at art galleries, and in basement improv venues. You're in a special place at a special moment in time, so be sure to draw from the resources surrounding you and contribute your own time, energy, and innovative thinking to this scene.

Finding Champions: Patrons, Partners, and Favorable Critics

As a Game Changer, you don't *need* the approval of others. You might not even *want* it! But, baby, it's cold outside, and when the public doesn't appreciate you, you'll want to warm yourself with the praise of a small circle of supporters.

William Shakespeare was fortunate to have royalty, Queen Elizabeth and King James I, as patrons who ensured his plays would make it to the stage. Poet Edna St. Vincent Millay had her dashing and nurturing husband, Eugen Boissevain, a Dutch importer and feminist who set out to provide her with a stable home life and relieve her of domestic duties so she could write. And director Arthur Penn, whose 1967 movie *Bonnie and Clyde* initially received mixed reviews, had movie critic Pauline Kael, who wrote a 7,000-word defense of the film for *The New Yorker*.

Lucky for painter Jackson Pollock, he had a loyal patron, a supportive partner, *and* a positive critic—all three.

As described in Chapter 1, "The A-Lister," Pollock became the first American painter to emerge from the long shadow cast by twentieth-century European artists like Pablo Picasso and Wassily Kandinsky. What made this possible, in part, was that he'd attained some level of success and had even caught the eye of Peggy Guggenheim, of *the* Guggenheims, who became his patron. In 1943, she commissioned a mural for her New York townhouse and gave Pollock free rein. But Pollock developed the painter's equivalent of writer's block. He struggled to find his own voice and develop his own style—a new, bold, American style.

The film *Pollock* (in which Ed Harris's resemblance to Pollock is uncanny) captures Pollock's frustration and despair and then the exhilaration of his breakthrough moment. After days of nothingness, days of staring at a blank canvas, inspiration strikes. Pollock lets loose, slapping—nearly stabbing—the huge canvas with paint in a frenzied state. The following morning, his future wife and fellow painter, the ever-tolerant Lee Krasner, finds Pollock asleep on the toilet as if he's so exhausted himself he can't move. She realizes he's done it. Her expression after she races down the hallway and witnesses the painting is priceless.

What she sees is an original painting with a not-so-original title, *Mural*: an eight-by-twenty-foot canvas teeming with energy. Its sheer scale and audacity took abstract expressionist painting to a new place and established Pollock as a leading artist.

So, Pollock had a wealthy patron and a supportive partner. What about a favorable critic? Yes, he had that, too. Clement Greenberg, who wrote for publications like the *Nation* and *Commentary*, was a resolute champion of Pollock's for a long time. He claimed he took one look at *Mural* and realized "Jackson was the greatest painter this country has produced."

Cautionary Tales for the Game Changer

Game Changer, you're blazing a new path in art and inviting others to accompany you. Let's look at some of the challenges you might face and those tendencies you can tame in order to hold strong to your vision.

Nurture Your Tendencies
Seek Supporters

As a Game Changer, you, probably more than any other creative type, need people around you to bolster and champion you when the going gets tough—and chances are, it will. Patrons aren't readily available, but you might have parents or a partner who will help out with some of the finances for a time while you try to make it in the arts. As for a champion, I bet you have friends or colleagues you could turn to who will understand what you're trying to do or have been in your place and can give you pep talks when you're feeling discouraged. And, don't forget the "you-scratch-my-back-and-I'll-scratch-yours" theory of promotion: "follow," "like," repost—do whatever it takes to boost others on social media sites and in online communities, and hopefully they will return the favor.

Patience Is an Elusive Virtue

Maybe you've got what others consider some harebrained creative scheme. You believe in your idea, but no one else seems to . . . yet. You're not going to be deterred by the reactions of others, Game Changer, but on the other hand, getting people to appreciate your art can require the perfect storm of your vision, the right timing, and the public's open-mindedness.

But sometimes the storm might not arrive for months or years or even longer. What's a Game Changer to do? Do you forge ahead despite the naysayers and hope you'll be described years from now as "ahead of your time"?

Creativity Booster
Naming Your Fears

Game Changers thrive on originality and want recognition for their visionary outlook. But being ahead of your time can mean you're all by yourself—and that can be scary. The first step toward overcoming, or at least making peace with, your fears is identifying them. Some fears common to Game Changers are:

- Being misunderstood
- Receiving rejections and harsh critiques
- Not achieving acceptance of your art within your lifetime
- Discovering that what you thought was an original concept has been done before
- Having to make compromises

See which of these resonate with you, and add three more of your fears to the list. Then, answer the question "What can I do?" for each one. For instance, if your worst fear is that you will receive rejection after rejection, write about what you could do to accept your fate—or change it—by bringing people around to your way of thinking. Repeat this exercise with your other fears, and see if it lessens the intensity of each one.

Or, do you track the storm with a meteorologist's precision so you can strike at just the right moment?

Striking at that moment is exactly what the writer Truman Capote did, and the result was the breakthrough book *In Cold Blood*, published in 1966 and still widely read decades later. It's considered the first full-length work of creative nonfiction, a type of writing in which the author uses all the hallmarks of great fiction—complex characters, revealing dialogue, vivid sensory descriptions—in writing about a true-life situation.

If you haven't read *In Cold Blood* yet, I urge you to get to a bookstore or online bookseller, pronto. It's riveting, in no small part because Capote brought this sensibility of a novelist, along with a novelist's sharpened tools, to the chilling story of multiple murders.

At the time, Capote was already a literary light known for his fiction, including *Breakfast at Tiffany's*. But he'd been plotting and planning a different approach to writing, which was sure to meet with resistance from official corners and the public. I can picture him, cartoonlike, rubbing his hands and licking his lips in anticipation of the chance to upend the worlds of literature and journalism.

And then the right opportunity arose—or, more accurately, Capote saw the opportunity and pounced on it. Capote read a short, easily overlooked newspaper article about the senseless murder of every member of the Clutter family in the middle of the night in their home in a remote part of Kansas. He wanted to investigate and report on the story behind the story. But, instead of treating the assignment in traditionally journalistic fashion, he spent six years interviewing the murderers and the townspeople who knew the Clutters. He then wrote about them the way authors write about fictional characters in a novel. Capote was an omniscient, godlike author, able to get inside people's heads, particularly when it came to the enigmatic murderer, Perry Edward Smith.

When Capote was asked by George Plimpton, writing in *The New York Times*, why he'd chosen to write about this crime in particular, he called the choice "altogether literary." He said, "The decision was based on a theory I've harbored since I first began to write professionally, which is well over 20 years ago. It seemed to me that journalism, reportage, could be forced to yield a serious new art form: the 'nonfiction novel,' as I thought of it."

Tame Your Tendencies
Cultivate Patience

Patience is not a natural tendency for Game Changers, but you'll have to learn to foster it if people don't rally behind you at first. Here are some approaches: Allow yourself to feel smug and superior to the "fools" who don't understand your vision (though I'd suggest keeping this to yourself). List your favorite writers, singers, or filmmakers whose work took time to find an audience, and take a look at it whenever you start to despair about your own prospects. Imagine the making of a documentary about you years or even decades from now, heralding you as a Game Changer. Any of these techniques will help stem your anxieties about ultimately attracting an audience.

Twenty years?

Capote continued, "When I first formed my theories concerning the nonfiction novel, many people with whom I discussed the matter were unsympathetic. They felt that what I proposed... was little more than a literary solution for fatigued novelists suffering from 'failure of imagination.' Personally, I felt that this attitude represented a 'failure of imagination' on their part."

Touché, Truman, touché.

You Can't Please All the Critics All the Time

If you're going to innovate, be prepared for pushback from critics. You can bypass professional reviewers by using social media, but official critics still wield a lot of influence and power. They can help boost your career, but they can also shut down a play after one night or cut into book or record sales or even instill doubts in you about your abilities. Don't let them!

Helen Vendler, a respected scholar and literary critic, acknowledged in the *Paris Review* that there are instances in which the experts, including her, don't appreciate poets who are ultimately regarded as brilliant. She said, "I fear giving short shrift to something that is really very good, which I don't recognize at the time. We all know critics who have done that: the critics of Keats who told him to go back to his apothecary pots; the critics of Stevens who thought he was a dandy; the critics of *The Waste Land* who thought it was a hoax; and perhaps, myself as a critic, say, of Pound, about whom I've never written, whom I think of as a minor poet of the *fin de siècle* and the early century." Ezra Pound, of course, turned out not to be minor at all.

So, remember, dear Game Changer, that the critics aren't always right. Also, bear in mind that your audience may be more receptive than the critics to experimentation. As author Jeanette Winterson observed of readers in an interview on CBS Radio's *Writers & Company*, "They will climb with you to the most unlikely places if they trust you, if the words give them the right footholds, the right handholds. That's what I want my readers to do: I want them to come with me when we're going mountain-climbing. This isn't a walk through a theme park. This is some dangerous place that neither of us has been before, and I hope that by traveling there first, I can encourage the reader to come with me and that we will make the trip again together, and safely."

Your colleagues might catch on before the critics, too. That was the case for comedian and writer Steve Martin. He describes how he arrived at his original form of stand-up comedy in his memoir *Born Standing Up: A Comic's Life*.

Even if you witnessed Martin perform on *Saturday Night Live* and in sold-out arenas, you might not have pinpointed what was so different about his brand of comedy, but you knew *something* was. *Born Standing Up* solves the mystery for us.

It surprised me to learn that it once was considered legit for stand-up comics to "borrow" and perform material from other comics, the way musicians do covers of others' songs. But, while Martin was a student at Long Beach State College, where he was an accomplished magician and an aspiring comic, he set a clear goal for himself: originality. He explains, "I would have to write everything in the act myself. Any line or idea with even a vague feeling of familiarity or provenance had to be expunged. There could be nothing that made the audience feel they weren't seeing something utterly new."

He was bothered by the predictability of one-liners ("How do you get to Carnegie Hall? Practice!"). *Ba-dum-dum*. It was as if the audience was being told what was funny and how to respond. Martin said to himself, "'What if there were no punch lines? What if there were no indicators?' ... The audience would eventually pick their own place to laugh, essentially out of desperation. This type of laugh seemed stronger to me, as they would be laughing at something *they chose*, rather than being told exactly when to laugh."

As is the case for so many Game Changers, it took a while for the critics to come around. In fact, one dismissed Martin as a "so-called comedian" and derided the absence of punch lines. Others disdained his happy feet, arrow-through-the-head antics. But friend and fellow comic Rick Moranis got it. He called Martin's approach "anti-comedy." And, eventually, Martin would become the first comedian to sell out Madison Square Garden for solo performances. *Victory!*

While some Game Changers, like Martin, take years to achieve recognition, others receive accolades from the critics early on. But, beware: critics can turn on you! That's what happened to poet E. E. Cummings.

When I was a kid, I thought Cummings was cool just because he didn't use capital letters. But, his unconventional forms go way beyond the superficial. What's been called his "playful tinkering with language" involved experimentations with form, punctuation, spelling, definitions, and syntax to arrive at an idiosyncratic style all his own.

These techniques were not mere gimmicks. Cummings scholar Norman Friedman writes in *E. E. Cummings: The Growth of a Writer* that this game-changing poet's innovations were attempts to strip the familiarity from language in order to strip the familiarity from the world at large. Or, as Friedman phrased it: "To transform the word is to transform the world."

Not surprisingly, the theme of many of Cummings's poems is the importance of being original, independent, and self-reliant. He was scornful of anyone who took refuge in conventional thinking. So it must have been galling to him when critics accused him of settling into his signature style and not "evolving" as an artist from the 1920s to the 1950s. The critic George Stade even called Cummings "a case of arrested development," writing, "He was a brilliant 20-year-old, but he remained merely precocious to the end of his life." Interestingly, the critic then acknowledged, "That may be one source of his appeal."

It seems you're damned if you do and damned if you don't! Be innovative and then abandon your innovation in favor of a new approach, the logic goes. Don't give in to such twisted logic. I say, be original, independent, and self-reliant, and if you are talented and lucky enough to hit upon a "signature style" that pleases you and moves art into new territory, you've earned the right to call yourself a Game Changer.

Creativity Booster
Handling Criticism

Anyone who claims they're not hurt by criticism is a damn liar. Artists and writers put so much effort—and so much of *themselves*—into their creative work that having it dismissed with one cutting remark in a review, on social media, or in a workshop is demoralizing. Believe me, I know. Years ago, one of my favorite professors said to me during a class break following a workshop of one of my short stories, "What were you *thinking?*" Ouch!

So, give in to the pain and even wallow in it for a few days. But, don't allow someone else's reaction to undermine your self-confidence or, worse, block you from doing what you love. You're a Game Changer, and you're on a mission!

Spotlight: Creators Who Survived Harsh Rejection

Criticism is tough enough, but there's nothing quite like outright rejection to test the mettle of a Game Changer. The pioneering work they do nearly screams "Reject me!" because it's bold and foreign and challenging.

Yet, for an ambitious Game Changer, rejection can be surprisingly motivating. Did you know that hip-hop artist, entrepreneur, and the king to Beyoncé's queen, **Jay Z**, was initially turned down by every label in the record industry? Rather than give up, he co-founded a record label, Roc-a-Fella Records, and produced his own records. And when the Italian knitwear designer Iceberg Apparel wouldn't offer him a decent endorsement deal even though he'd literally been singing their praises in verse and boosting their sales, he started a competing clothing line, Rocawear, and sold it ten years later for over $200 million. There's nothing quite as sweet as rejecting the rejecters and succeeding against all odds.

For those who receive a rejection in the form of a letter or email, it can especially sting since the words aimed at you are right there in black and white, unavoidable. And yet, the dreaded rejection letter is a staple of life for many a Game Changer. If you receive one or two or three or ninety-nine for your manuscript or record demo, try not to get too discouraged. To make you feel better, here are rejection letters received by great writers and artists before they achieved fame. Read them when you're in the doldrums, and you'll instantly feel better.

A little novel you might have heard of, *Moby Dick*, written by **Herman Melville** and published in 1851, received this hilarious suggestion from publisher Peter J. Bentley: "First, we must ask, does it have to be a whale? While this is a rather delightful, if somewhat esoteric, plot device, we recommend an antagonist with a more popular visage among the younger readers. For instance, could not the Captain be struggling with a depravity towards young, perhaps voluptuous, maidens?"

Writer **Gertrude Stein** received a rejection letter from publisher Arthur Fifield in 1912 that mimicked her unusual—and unusually repetitive—style. It read: "Dear Madam, I am only one, only one, only one. Only one being, one at the same time. Not two, not three, only one. Only one life to live, only sixty minutes in one hour. Only one pair of eyes. Only one brain. Only one being. Being only one, having only one pair of eyes, having only one time, having only one life, I cannot read your M.S. three or four times. Not even one time. Only one look, only one look is enough. Hardly one copy would sell here. Hardly one. Hardly one. Sincerely Yours, A.C. Fifield."

Guess who penned a rejection letter to **George Orwell** for *Animal Farm*? Fellow writer T. S. Eliot! And this was the very novel Orwell felt achieved the balance between art and political message he was striving for (read more about this in Chapter 5, "The Activist"). Eliot, the editor at the publishing firm Faber & Faber at the time, apparently disagreed, stating Orwell did not elicit enough sympathy for his anti-Fascist cause and telling him, "Your pigs are far more intelligent than the other animals, and therefore the best qualified to run the farm—in fact, there couldn't have been an *Animal Farm* at all without them: so that what was needed (someone might argue), was not more communism but more public-spirited pigs."

Building on the popularity of *Monty Python's Flying Circus*, British comedian **John Cleese** cowrote another television series, *Fawlty Towers*, which eventually aired on the BBC, but not until after it was rejected by the television station's comedy script editor. Here's the letter: "I'm afraid I thought this one as dire as its title.... A collection of clichés and stock characters which I can't see being anything but a disaster." *Fawlty Towers* went on to become one of the BBC's most popular sitcoms.

Superstar author **Stephen King** received the following response to his first novel, *Carrie:* "We are not interested in science fiction which deals with negative utopias. They do not sell." The book was rejected so many times, King speared the letters on a spike in his bedroom. *Carrie* was finally published in 1974 with a print run of 30,000 copies. When the paperback version was released a year later, it sold over one million copies in twelve months.

Jim Lee is an artist, writer, and copublisher of DC Comics. But when he was starting out, his drawings were rejected by Marvel editor Eliot R. Brown, who wrote, "Your work looks as if it were done by four different people. Your best pencils are on page 7, panel with agents, and close up of the face. The rest of the pencils are of much weaker quality. The same can be said for your inking.

Resubmit when your work is consistent and when you have learned to draw hands."

Following the mega-success of her *Harry Potter* series, **J. K. Rowling** decided to pitch her next book, a postwar detective novel, *The Cuckoo's Calling*, under the pseudonym Robert Galbraith. She received rejection letters from British publishers Crème de la Crime and Constable and Robinson, with an executive from the latter firm predicting the book would be a commercial flop. Seeking to be helpful, they offered advice on how to succeed in the future, including counseling "Galbraith" to look up advice in a magazine writing guide, join a writers' group or take a course, and not give away the ending of the book when pitching it. The book proceeded to top Amazon's best-sellers list and received critical claim, and plans are under way for a TV series. Don't you wonder if that exec kept their job?

Tame Your Tendencies
Learn to Reject Rejection

It should go without saying, Game Changer, but I'll say it anyway: you cannot allow rejection to dissuade or derail you. If you receive constructive criticism, see if it resonates with you and make changes as you see fit. But, never forget that what you're doing might make people uncomfortable or threaten their risk-averse nature. So, if you receive a rejection letter or email, do the following: Burn it, frame it, delete it, spear it, tear it up, or save it so you can later send it back to the rejecter with a note saying, "I told you so." And, most important: send your writing to other publications, audition for other parts, approach a different record label—just don't give up!

The Takeaway

If you're a Game Changer or someone with Game Changer tendencies, you're determined to break down barriers and open up new possibilities for art. What can you do to make the most of your rebel spirit—and keep your spirits up—while waiting for others to accept and applaud your ideas and innovations?

- Stay true to your vision and don't compromise for the sake of acceptance, money, or other rewards.
- Make sure you're a rebel *with* a cause and not just crashing convention because it's fun or feeds your ego.
- Break away from tradition but acknowledge that prior works of art served as a catalyst for you.
- Take pride in yourself as an individualist, but also be open to becoming part of a scene or movement, too.
- Be prepared for the possibility that you might have to wait years—even decades—for your ideas to be accepted.
- Learn to expect and deal with rejection and criticism—you're probably going to be on the receiving end of it, but you can rise above it.

Chapter 4

THE SENSITIVE SOUL: EXPRESSING YOURSELF AND HELPING OTHERS

~~~

Sometimes I wonder how all those who do not write, compose,
or paint can manage to escape the madness, melancholia,
the panic and fear which is inherent in a human situation.

—GRAHAM GREENE, *WAYS OF ESCAPE*

Is the phrase "I feel your pain" more than just an empty saying to you? Instead, is it more like your motto?

Rainy days and Mondays may bring other people down, but not you. Or, sure, they bring you down, but they also get your creative juices flowing.

Maybe when you were a kid and your Mom was depressed, you could make her smile by cracking a joke. Or, when you were a tween, you discovered that writing a blog post made you feel less alone. Or, these days, singing at the top of your lungs in the shower releases inner tension just as the hot water releases the tension in your muscles.

You just might be a Sensitive Soul.

Why Do Sensitive Souls Create?

If you're a Sensitive Soul or have Sensitive Soul tendencies, you feel things deeply. And, instead of keeping those emotions contained, you turn to creative outlets. This may not be a matter of choice for you—it may instead be a true need. Here are some of the reasons why you most likely create.

Because when you were little, if a kid in the neighborhood called you a crybaby or your brother gave you two-for-flinching, you'd run to your room and slam the door or throw yourself onto your bed and cry (thus proving the neighbor kid right). But not for long. You'd feel so much better after writing a poem about the cruelty of others or doing a crayon drawing of your brother where you gave him really big ears and beady eyes.

Because you don't understand how people can say things like "Whatev." How can they be so Zen? Everything gets you stirred up, and, truth be told, most days you prefer it that way. Besides, you're not immune to happiness—there are times when you hear your baby gurgle or your boyfriend tells you he's in love with you or you catch the last glimpse of the crimson sun before it slips into the sea, and you're filled with joy. You can't wait to capture this fleeting feeling. Because you had a messed-up childhood and you know the only way you're going to free yourself from its very long tentacles is to make a very short film about it. Because nothing feels better than bringing someone you love out of their misery by singing a song to them or writing them a love poem.

Snapshot of a Sensitive Soul

Sensitive Souls may be thin-skinned, but such sensitivity also extends to others. You don't just listen to your friends, you empathize with them. And, this enhanced capacity for feeling comes through in your art.

Who's most likely to write a play that will take an audience's collective hearts and smash them to bits? Or leave a reader weeping at the end of a novel yet wishing for more? Or compose a violin concerto that will transport listeners back to their childhoods, the first time they felt loved, or the beautiful dream they never wanted to awaken from? A Sensitive Soul, of course!

But a lot of famous Sensitive Souls weren't just sensitive. Words like "tortured" or "tormented" are used to describe them— and there's good reason for that. Untreated or poorly treated depression or bipolar disorder might have been the root cause of many well-known artists' suffering. On the flip side, those mood disorders may have also contributed to those artists' creativity.

When Sensitive Souls use art to bring themselves some relief from suffering, they also help others escape their pain. When Sensitive Souls use art to fill in the missing parts of their histories, they also help others assemble the puzzle of their lives. A memoir, a self-portrait, a novel that's a "thinly disguised" story of the author's life? Millions of people might see their own lives reflected in the self-reflective art of the Sensitive Soul.

Change the art world or the political world through creativity? As a Sensitive Soul, you'll leave these aims to others. You're too busy coping with and making meaning of your life and helping others do the same through your art.

Varieties of Sensitive Souls

You might be the kind of Sensitive Soul who seeks to make sense of certain life experiences or achieve some catharsis. Or, you might be the sort of Sensitive Soul who wants to help others escape their

Artistic Personality Quiz
So, You Think You're a Sensitive Soul

1. Do you need to pour out all the feelings inside you through some creative outlet?
2. Have you been called "oversensitive" more times than you care to recall?
3. Would you choose a life of the highest highs and the lowest lows over an "ordinary" one?
4. Do you find that when you're in a state of melancholy or when you're feeling a little manic, you're also spurred on, creatively?
5. Did you realize from a young age that you could make other people (a depressed parent, for instance) feel better by "performing" or giving them a picture you drew?
6. When you're feeling down, does expressing yourself artistically lift your spirits or even feel lifesaving?
7. Do you do creative work based on your own life to try to make more sense of things for yourself and possibly to make others feel less alone?
8. Do you sometimes choose projects that will allow you to collaborate or in some other way connect with people?
9. Are you determined to record every precious moment of life so you never have to let them go?

If you answered "yes" to most of these questions, you are a Sensitive Soul. And, if you answered "yes" to even a few of these questions, you have some strong Sensitive Soul tendencies. Either way, read on.

suffering. These are some of the traits that differentiate one Sensitive Soul from another.

See the Sidebar for a list of varieties, and read on for an exploration of some of the most common ones.

The Emoter

As a Sensitive Soul, you have so many feelings roiling around inside you—love, sadness, angst, joy—that your cup runneth over, and the contents *have* to spill out.

There are times when you curse your sensitive nature. How come everyone else is going about their business while you can't stop thinking about your lying ex? Or how you shouldn't bring a

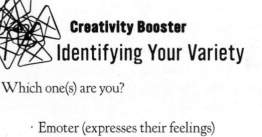

Creativity Booster
Identifying Your Variety

Which one(s) are you?

- Emoter (expresses their feelings)
- Intensifier (experiences great intensity of emotions)
- Tormented Artist (connects creativity with suffering)
- Flight Attendant (wants their art to help themselves and others)
- Survivor (believes art has saved them)
- Meaning Maker (makes sense of loss or tragedy)
- Connector (uses art to feel connected to others)
- Recorder (tries to capture every moment of life)

child into the world while there are millions of refugee children who are homeless. Or whether you hurt your daughter with that comment about her haircut.

Other times you feel grateful that you can still be moved to tears by the sappy ending of a rom-com or enthralled with the sparkling meteor shower overhead or connected to your child so deeply, it makes your heart hurt.

Luckily, you have an amazing outlet for feelings that might otherwise consume you. You don't have to hold it all in. You get to take all your sadness or angst or exhilaration and pour it into a song, a painting, or a blog post.

Creativity is your outlet. Creativity is your cure.

Your emotionality is the source of your creativity, Sensitive Soul, so don't stifle it. Writer and diarist Anaïs Nin believed this to her core. When her seventeen-year-old nephew told her he wanted to become an author, she wrote him a letter cautioning him to give in to—not avoid—what others might call an overabundance of emotion. She wrote, "You must not fear, hold back, count or be a miser with your thoughts and feelings. . . . Permit yourself to flow and overflow, allow for the rise in temperature, all the expansions and intensifications. Something is always born of excess: great art was born of great terrors, great loneliness, great inhibitions, instabilities, and it always balances them."

It turns out this flowing and overflowing of emotions may not always be a matter of choice for some people. Research shows it may be an involuntary response growing out of a basic biological need: the need to communicate.

When neurologist Alice Flaherty of Massachusetts General Hospital gave birth to stillborn twins, she found that in her grief she could not stop writing, writing, writing. She wrote up and down her arm and over and under any piece of paper within reach. This condition even has a name: hypergraphia. Later, Flaherty thought back on her unusual reaction to shock and grief and was curious why she'd responded like that. She formulated the "need theory of self-expression," explored in her book *The Midnight Disease*, which states that while writing is not a primary need like eating, breathing, or sleeping, it *is* a secondary need. And it stems from the same biological urge that causes someone to cry out in sorrow or anger.

George Orwell called this urge to express oneself creatively "a demon whom one can neither resist nor understand," and writes, "for all one knows that is simply the same instinct that makes a baby squall for attention."

Well, maybe Orwell's right when he calls our urges "demonic" because they're not within our control. But, Sensitive Soul, when it comes to creativity, control isn't really the point, is it? Self-expression is.

The Intensifier

You might think gloom and doom are the twin engines driving creativity. But what about joy? Happiness? A love of life, romance, nature? Can't you be just as moved to create out of happiness as sadness? To take a picture of the harvest moon peeking through the clouds, choreograph a lip dub video, or write a song that incites wild dancing—all out of an exuberance for life?

We all know songs that *had* to have been written in a state of delight. In my iTunes library, I've got a playlist cleverly titled "Boppy Singles." Some of my favorites? "I Feel the Earth Move" by Carole King, "Can't Keep It In" by Cat Stevens, "September" by Earth, Wind & Fire, "Hey Ya" by OutKast, and early Beatles songs galore, from "She Loves You" to "I Saw Her Standing There" to so many more. I bet you know the sort of song I mean—one that exudes joy.

Now I'm picturing paintings like Monet's poppy fields, which capture the pure hues of flowers and the brilliance of sunlight and make me exhale with deep satisfaction. I'm also remembering my parents taking my sister and me to Lincoln Center to see Rudolf Nureyev soar above the stage higher than I ever would have imagined a mortal being could. Didn't all of these come from a happy, hopeful spirit within their creators?

And yet, happiness gets a bad rap when it comes to creativity. Some people associate "meaningful" art with sad states and "simplistic" art with happiness. In *Art as Therapy*, Alain de Botton and John Armstrong write that people tend to equate pretty pictures with a sort of sentimentality considered the enemy of complexity. Such pictures are said to present an idealized version of life that disguises reality as it is and enables people to live in denial. (And what, exactly, is the problem with that?!)

Creativity can and does spring from both sorrow and joy. And, as Flaherty points out, from a neurological standpoint, pleasure and pain systems do not cancel each other out; they coexist. Simply put, joy and suffering are two sides of the same coin.

The singer Adele acknowledged this connection in an interview on the *Today* show in which she reflected on how it felt to write her breakup—and breakout—album, *21*. She said, "I don't think sadness is always devastating. It can be quite uplifting and joyful as well, and sometimes you have to let yourself be sad in order to move forward." When you listen to "Someone Like You," I'm sure you can hear Adele's pain, but don't you also hear an anthem of defiance and even some hope?

Flaherty says joy and sadness are each the opposite of *blandness*, the true creativity killer. Research supports her perspective, with studies showing that when it comes to creative motivation, it's not so much *which* emotion you're feeling as the *intensity* of the emotion.

I've seen this theory of intensity play out among my creative writing students. When any of them struggles with issues of

Creativity Booster
Create from Any Emotion

If you're someone who only feels inspired to create when you're going through a painful time—a breakup, your grandmother's death, a rejection letter—try the flip side. Let yourself feel inspired by the first sighting of a crocus after a harsh winter, a new crush, or a positive review. Sit with the image of the crocus, recording your thoughts as they arise. Or try out a new color palette that symbolizes your crush. See what it feels like when joy instead of sadness is your muse. And, vice versa: if you're someone who usually creates out of happiness but is afraid of what will come up for you if you do so from a sad or angry state, give it a try. You might find it too difficult for now, but, then again, you might find it freeing.

craft—voice, structure, scene setting—that's to be expected. But any time an aspiring writer says he or she can't think of anything to write about, that worries me. It could be a sign they're not throwing themselves into the messiness of life, which is the source of so much rich material, the source of intense feelings that stir the creative pot, at least for a Sensitive Soul.

So, if you find yourself wanting for material, you might follow author William Saroyan's advice to writers (and, by extension, all artists) in *The Daring Young Man on the Flying Trapeze*: "When you laugh, laugh like hell, and when you get angry, get good and angry. Try to be alive." And, I'd add, use these emotional states to mine material for your art.

The Tormented Artist

The stereotype of the "tormented artist" is a persistent one. There's something strangely romantic about the loner, the mad genius, the sufferer who transforms pain into masterpieces. But, the truth is, emotional or mental suffering has led many of our most revered artists to take their own lives or to die from a drug or alcohol overdose, often at a young age: Virginia Woolf, Sylvia Plath, Judy Garland, Mark Rothko, Diane Arbus, Jimi Hendrix, Janice Joplin, Kurt Cobain, David Foster Wallace, Amy Winehouse... the list is long.

We tell ourselves these artists were too pure and sensitive to survive in this world. But that's not the full story. Throughout the centuries, artists themselves have held up suffering as a state to aspire to for the sake of art. The poet John Berryman, for one, even claimed in a *Paris Review* interview, "The artist is extremely lucky who is presented with the worst possible ordeal which will not actually kill him."

Some renowned creators were so single-mindedly devoted to their art—oftentimes to the detriment of their mental and physical health, relationships, or finances—that, given the option of a "happy life" or brilliant art, they chose art. They believed they needed a life of high drama or near tragedies or grand visions to inspire them to their artistic heights.

Edvard Munch, best known as the painter of *The Scream*, felt this way. The story behind his iconic painting is revealing: an ominous vision came to Munch as he stood one day on the edge of the Oslofjord, an inlet in the southeast of Norway. In his words, "The sun began to set—suddenly the sky turned blood red. I stood there trembling with anxiety—and I sensed an endless scream passing through nature." Munch believed his anxiety was essential to his creativity, writing in his diary, "My fear of life is necessary to me, as is my illness. They are indistinguishable from me, and their destruction would destroy my art."

High drama might have driven Berryman and Munch, but be careful about fully buying into their pronouncements. After all, if you invite suffering in, it will gladly oblige you. Writer Mary Karr, who has revealed her battles with depression and alcoholism in her series of memoirs, beginning with *The Liars' Club*, agrees with this, saying in *Salon*, "I think being tortured as a virtue is a kind of antiquated sense of what it is to be an artist. It comes out of that Symbolist idea, back to Rimbaud and all that disordering of the senses and all of that being in some exalted state. When I've been that way, I've always been less exalted than I would have liked."

The Flight Attendant

The avant-garde dramatist Antonin Artaud once said, "Art first heals the artist and subsequently helps heal others." I think of this as the flight attendant theory of creativity. You know when the flight attendant instructs that, in an emergency, you should put the oxygen mask on yourself first and then put one on your child? Well, that's because you have to ensure your own welfare before you can help others. The same goes for creativity.

The desire to benefit others through your art is not purely altruistic; there's even some of the A-Lister's MO in anyone who's hoping their art is so compelling it will make people roar with laughter or blink back tears or be brought to their feet at a performance. But Sensitive Souls also want their audience to leave the theater or the last page of a novel feeling less alone, better understood, or even inspired to make their own art.

The writer Leo Tolstoy went even further, describing how an artist could not just *affect* others, but also *infect* an audience with the creator's own feelings. While that sounds more than a little unsanitary, when he spoke of the infectiousness of art, he described it in hallowed terms, writing in *What Is Art?*, "The receiver of a true artistic impression is so united to the artist that he feels as if the work were his own and not someone else's—as if what it expresses were just what he had long been wishing to express."

I wouldn't be surprised if a lot of people felt this way the night of the 2016 Academy Awards when Lady Gaga took to the stage to sing "'Til It Happens to You," the song she cowrote with Diane Warren for the documentary film about sexual assault, *The Hunting Ground*. Gaga had been raped when she was nineteen, and so it was clear the song had a personal meaning for her. While her all-white outfit and white piano were stunning, gone were the outrageous get-ups Gaga is known for. In their place was a raw and pained but uplifting performance that blew the audience away, especially when Gaga was joined onstage by a group of fifty survivors of sexual assault, who sang in solidarity with her and held signs identifying the specific nature of their horrific experiences. The commanding performance captured what some sexual assault survivors had been feeling and possibly keeping inside for years.

Do you, too, have something you've wanted to express through song, dance, poetry, or other outlets for a long time? Take a chance and do something creative to help heal yourself, Sensitive Soul, and in the process you just might help others to heal, too.

Positive Tendencies of Sensitive Souls

Saving Yourself Through Art

Artists throughout the centuries have praised the curative powers of creativity, saying it prevented them from sinking into scary depths, made life livable, or even outright saved their lives.

Author Sherwood Anderson told his son, an aspiring artist, "The object of art is not to make salable pictures. It is to save yourself." Robert Lowell mused in a poem whether getting well is an art or art a way of getting well. Poet Anne Sexton said, "Poetry led me by the hand out of madness." And author Jeanette Winterson writes, "Art saved me; it got me through my depression and self-loathing, back to a place of innocence." Writer Thomas Williams put it more directly: "I write so I don't die before I'm dead."

Suffering is inevitable, so the central questions for you, as a Sensitive Soul, are these: Can you transform your suffering into art? And, in doing so, can you transform—and even save—yourself? Here are some examples of artists who proved they could answer both questions in the affirmative.

In Alain de Botton's literary self-help book, *How Proust Can Change Your Life*, he examined what we can learn from the writer and notorious hypochondriac Marcel Proust about "suffering successfully." Proust was quite a character: sickly, neurotic, attached (some might say too attached) to his mother, and closeted. But as de Botton reminds us, suffering on its own has never been responsible for producing art. Most people struggle with difficulties in their lives, but not everyone who struggles can turn their painful experiences into an aria or stanza. Not so for Proust, who tapped into his suffering to write the seven-volume opus *In Search of Lost Time*. Creating art from anguish grants it meaning and can make life worthwhile for the sufferer.

Yayoi Kusama, an avant-garde artist from Japan, has testified to the lifesaving power of art. When Kusama was young and still living in Tokyo, she sent a letter to her idol, Georgia O'Keeffe. One day, after Kusama had moved to New York, the famous painter came to see how her admirer was doing. O'Keeffe introduced Kusama to an art dealer who then bought one of her paintings, and her career started to take off.

But, there's more to Kusama's story. As she described it in *The Telegraph*, "I suffered from hallucinations, and making art helped ease the shock. Painting saved my life: when I wanted to commit suicide, my doctor encouraged me to paint more. I fight pain, anxiety and fear every day, and art is the only method I have found to relieve my illness."

In the memoir *Townie*, writer Andre Dubus III recounts his hardscrabble childhood and adolescence in the mill town of Haverhill, Massachusetts, after his parents divorced and his famous author father abandoned his kids. Dubus got into street fighting and boxing until he discovered writing. Here's how he describes his experience to *Writer's Digest*: "It was a semi-spiritual, life-saving moment where I found something that just made me feel like me, and that was not destructive. I don't want to paint the picture that I was some badass who discovered creativity—it was more it was always in me."

Writer Augusten Burroughs, whose highly unusual upbringing formed the basis for his memoir and the movie based on it, *Running with Scissors*, spent much of his life as an alcoholic until he discovered an activity even more addictive than drinking—and that activity was writing. In his third in a series of memoirs, *Lust & Wonder*, he describes being in a state of complete creative immersion when writing his first book, the novel *Sellevision*. He wrote it in a nearly uninterrupted outpouring (a state called "flow" that's described in Chapter 2, "The Artisan"). As he phrases it, "Writing carried me much further away from myself than drinking had ever managed to do." And with his dry humor, Burroughs further writes, "This should be a criminal activity, punishable by imprisonment or worse. The feeling it gave me was larger than the feeling of drunk."

As a Sensitive Soul, you know for yourself what creativity does for your mental health. You've hopefully found that doing anything from designing your flower garden to experimenting with different drum sounds on GarageBand has made you feel better.

Everyone has something to express, and everyone, at any age, can benefit from expressing it. When people find out I teach personal essay writing, they sometimes question what a young person could possibly have lived through that would be worth writing about. I answer: you'd be amazed. Multiple homicides within a family; incest; food disorders; self-harm and cutting; a parent with early-onset Alzheimer's; the death of a mother or father or grandparent; and all the other, more expected milestones that are the stuff of life for someone in their late teens or early twenties. I hope and believe that writing about their difficulties and putting them out there for others to read brings my students some relief and makes them feel less alone.

Research, in fact, confirms that creativity has healing powers. Making art is good for you, mind, body, and soul. In 2010, researchers did an analysis published in the *American Journal of Public Health* of more than one hundred studies on the impact of art on your health and your ability to heal yourself. The studies covered everything from music and writing to dance and the visual arts, and each study examined more than thirty patients who were battling chronic illness and cancer.

When patients did visual arts (painting, drawing, photography, pottery, and textiles), they benefited in a variety of measurable ways. It distracted them from their illness, decreased negative emotions and increased positive ones, and even improved medical outcomes. It specifically reduced depression, stress, and anxiety and enhanced spontaneity, expressions of grief, positive identity, and social networks. In another study, published in *Psychosomatic Medicine* in 2004, this one involving HIV patients, researchers found that the act of writing positively affected the patients' health *at a cellular level* and boosted their immune system. In other words, the benefits of doing art are not all in your head.

Doing creative projects is beneficial for people as they age, too. In 2001, the results of a study conducted by the National Endowment for the Arts, in collaboration with The George Washington

Nurture Your Tendencies
Reflect on Feeling Better

Think about a time when doing something creative gave you a much-needed lift. Try to remember an instance when you made a delicious hash from Thanksgiving leftovers or doodled in class or sang in the shower. Not all creativity has to have a larger goal. See if you can incorporate such small, uplifting creative acts into your week here and there, just as you might meditation or exercise.

University, showed that older people who participated in community arts programs were happier, healthier (both physically and mentally), and had longer life expectancies than those who didn't.

So, Sensitive Soul, if you've ever said that doing art or music or dance has saved you, you weren't exaggerating.

Finding Meaning in Loss

To loosely paraphrase Jane Austen, it is a truth universally acknowledged that losing someone you love is devastating. There are no two ways about it. And so it's no surprise that loss through death or betrayal is an epic theme of drama, film, song, and literature stretching back to art's very beginnings. As a Sensitive Soul, you might want to express raw, unfiltered emotion, as Kurt Cobain did on Nirvana's "Where Did You Sleep Last Night?" in the band's acoustic performance on MTV. While the song dates back to at least the 1870s, no version is quite like Nirvana's, where Cobain unleashes his pain in a chilling primal scream of a song.

Responding to a recent painful incident in your life can result in art that's potent and visceral. After some time and with a little distance, you might also want to start a project that allows you to reflect on—not just react to—a devastating experience. Marcel Proust believed that "griefs, at the moment when they change into ideas, lose some of their power to injure our heart." These writers discovered the truth of Proust's observation.

Poet and nonfiction writer Meghan O'Rourke wrote a memoir, *The Long Goodbye*, about mourning her mother, who died young of colorectal cancer. O'Rourke said in an interview with *The New York Times*, "As her disease progressed, I found myself writing down all the experiences we had.... It helped me externalize what was happening. After she died, I kept writing—and reading—trying to understand or just get a handle on grief, which was different from what I thought it would be." O'Rourke called this writing "a kind of stay against dread, and chaos."

Cheryl Strayed has also tried to come to terms with the loss of her mother at a young age, what she calls her "genesis story," through her novel *Torch* and her wildly popular memoir, *Wild*. In *Torch*, the daughter, Claire, acknowledges how she'd "never done this before—basked in the glory of her mother's death, of her own orphan story." Claire also says, "It felt dirty and cruel and yet also like a complete relief, as if her grief really had passed away from her entirely now, as if her life was only a story that she could hold up for display."

Nora Ephron, who was famously cheated on by her famous journalist-husband, came to terms with a different kind of grief—one accompanied by a potent emotion: fury. In her roman à clef, *Heartburn*, the heroine (and Nora stand-in), Rachel, is asked, "Why do you feel like you have to turn everything into a story?" She responds, "Because if I tell the story, I control the version. Because if I tell the story, I can make you laugh, and I would rather you laugh at me than feel sorry for me. Because if I tell the story, it doesn't hurt as much. Because if I tell the story, I can get on with it."

It's the getting on with it that is one of the greatest gifts creativity can give to you and other Sensitive Souls when you're trying to rebound from a terrible loss.

Coping, Creatively, with Isolation

You might go through periods in your life when you're on your own a lot, for whatever reason, and the feelings of isolation get to you. This can be especially tough on a Sensitive Soul. Maybe working from home seemed like an awesome idea ... until you realized you actually miss all the conversations at the office about who's binge-watching what. Or, maybe you were looking forward to having a college roommate, but it turns out you're living alone most of the time because she's basically moved in with her boyfriend. Or, you might have a physical disability or illness that prevents you from getting out as much as you'd like.

Feeling isolated or lonely can be hard, and creativity is certainly not going to fully compensate for a lack of companionship. But, aloneness can serve as the impetus to do something creative as well as the time to devote to it. It also frees you to do something that's rare in an overly scheduled, device-addicted society: use your imagination. These artists certainly scored by allowing their isolation to feed their imaginations.

At the age of nine, director Francis Ford Coppola was stricken by polio an unlucky year before the vaccine was discovered. He became partially paralyzed and couldn't walk or even move his left arm. How's a young boy supposed to pass the time when he's stuck in bed for a whole year, not even knowing if he'll ever fully recover? If you're the future director of one of cinema's most revered and highly ranked films, *The Godfather*, you experiment with your father's tape recorder and a 16mm toy projector, of course! Coppola spent countless hours trying to make soundtracks for Mickey Mouse movies and other films he could project on a screen at home. "Seems like much of my youth was spent trying to synchronize sound to picture," Coppola wryly observed when he was interviewed on *Inside the Actors Studio*.

When asked if confinement and solitude were important factors in his development as an artist, Coppola answered with an unequivocal yes. As he said, "I just kind of cooked up a fantasy world for myself, and I would imagine that was the beginning of the same fantasy world that I occupy right now."

Richard Starkey, a.k.a. Ringo Starr, was what used to be called a "sickly" child, afflicted twice by life-threatening illnesses. When he was just six, he was hospitalized with appendicitis, which led to an infection that sent him into a coma. When his sickness kept him out of school for nearly a year, he fell behind academically, and he started to feel alienated and isolated from his peers. To keep him occupied during one of his hospital stays, his parents bought him two toys: a little red bus and a small drum. Little Richie, as he was then known, was, as you might have guessed, enamored of the drum. But in the "no good deed is left unpunished" category, when he leaned over to give the bus to the boy in the next bed, the future drummer of the Beatles fell on his head and knocked himself out!

Five years later, he contracted tuberculosis and had to recover in a sanatorium (which was then called by the more pleasant-sounding name "greenhouse") in the country for nearly two years. The caretakers gave the patients lessons once a week in skills ranging from household chores to arts and crafts to musical instruments. The drum lessons changed the trajectory of Ringo's life. He never returned to school, preferring instead to stay at home and listen to music while keeping a beat by hitting biscuit tins with sticks. He took odd jobs and then joined bands that ultimately led to his discovery by John, Paul, and George. The rest, as they say, is rock 'n' roll history.

We can't know for sure if any of these artists would have become icons without those lonely, isolated times during their childhoods. But, we can probably say their misfortune provided them with the rare chance to let loose their imagination and discover doing something they loved—something that saved them from boredom and ennui and loneliness and maybe even hopelessness.

Spotlight: Frida Kahlo, Painting to Overcome Isolation

Frida Kahlo, the famous Mexican painter, suffered tremendously in her life: polio at age seven; a near-fatal accident resulting in a broken spine, collarbone, and pelvis and a crushed right leg and foot at eighteen; chronic pain; being encased in orthopedic corsets and plaster casts for months at a time; ulcers on her right foot, which was ultimately amputated shortly before she died. She underwent no fewer than thirty-five operations throughout her adult life and was often confined to a wheelchair or her bed. But, remarkably, she kept painting through it all. Can you even imagine the torment of her life if she didn't have a creative outlet?

In the introduction to *The Diary of Frida Kahlo*, writer and fellow Mexican Carlos Fuentes says that Kahlo, through her unyielding spirit, shows everyone that "suffering could not wither, nor sickness stale, her infinite variety." He also writes, "She directly describes her own pain, it does not render her mute, her scream is articulate because it achieves a visible and emotional form."

Of the 143 paintings Kahlo did, 55 are self-portraits, and while they're colorful and vibrant and wildly imaginative, she also did not shy away from showing herself in constraints and braces, stuck in a wheelchair, or with her internal organs exposed. Painting herself as she was rather than as she wished she could be helped Kahlo come to terms with her terrible predicament. As she wrote in her journal, "Anguish and pain, pleasure and death are no more than a process."

In an article about Kahlo in *The Boston Globe*, Sebastian Smee comments, "The idea that art can do this—mainlining rawest emotions, transmuting hurt, physical suffering, and psychic slush into the pictorial equivalent of hard-packed rubies and sapphires—has inspired more people to take up art than anyone could count." In the process of keeping herself going, Kahlo showed the rest of us how to rise above our circumstances by making art.

Nurture Your Tendencies
Overcome Isolation

What do most people do to pass the time when they're feeling too secluded, even if it's just for a few days while they're under the weather? Turn to their devices, of course! Obsessively check social media sites. Compulsively text. Follow the lives of their "friends" by watching reality TV shows. And there's no doubt all of this helps. But, what if the next time you're in seclusion with your chicken soup and your smartphone, you also wrote in a journal for an hour each day? Or when your partner's away for a few days, you did some charcoal or pastel drawings in a sketch pad? I guarantee you it will distract you from your misery, make the time pass more quickly, and maybe even be the catalyst for your next creative project.

Paying It Forward

If you're a Sensitive Soul, you can probably think of times when a play or concert or novel left its mark on you, a permanent tattoo. You're grateful to be so deeply affected, and this gratitude is, in part, what makes you want to do the same for others. Singer Mary J. Blige, for one, has had this experience.

When I think of a performer who sings from her core, and whose singing infects others in the way Leo Tolstoy described, it's Blige. But, before she became a singer, her life was turned around by other performers' music. She even called her 2010–2011 world concert tour the "Music Saved My Life Tour."

Blige survived a tough childhood in the Bronx: She was raised by a mother suffering from alcoholism and abandoned by a father who was a Vietnam War veteran with PTSD and who physically abused her mother. Blige was sexually abused at a young age and later became addicted to drugs, alcohol, and sex. Music is what made the difference in her life.

Blige said in an interview with SFGate, "Music makes us want to live. You don't know how many times people have told me that they'd been down and depressed and just wanted to die. But then a special song caught their ear and that helped give them renewed strength. That's the power music has. I believe there are certain things that God uses to get us out of a bad situation, and I believe music was one of the things he used for me. The first time I heard 'Keep on Moving' by Soul II Soul, I felt like somebody pumped a new spirit in me that made me want to go on." In her own singing, as well as her philanthropy, Blige seeks to do the same for others, especially women who are trying to rise out of poverty or abuse or even that most universal of experiences: heartbreak.

Music has a demonstrable ability to heal the brain and heart, as neurologist and author Oliver Sacks describes in his book

Musicophilia. He captures music's unique impact on a person, writing, "Music can pierce the heart directly. It needs no mediation. One does not have to know anything about Dido and Aeneas [characters in Henry Purcell's namesake opera, from 1689] to be moved by her lament for him. Everyone who has ever lost someone knows what Dido is expressing. And there is, finally, a deep and mysterious paradox here, for while such music makes one experience pain and grief more intensely, it brings solace and consolation at the same time."

That would be a pretty good legacy, wouldn't it, if you managed through your music or another art form to bring solace and consolation both to yourself and to others?

There's a self-serving (though not selfish) aspect to helping people through your art, too. Writer James Baldwin believed the only value in suffering is to help others suffer less, telling congregants at New York City's Community Church in 1962: "You must understand that your pain is trivial except insofar as you can use it to connect with other people's pain; and insofar as you can do that with your pain, you can be released from it, and then hopefully it works the other way around, too; insofar as I can tell you what it is to suffer, perhaps I can help you to suffer less."

Kenny Porpora, author of the memoir *The Autumn Balloon*, which tackles a trifecta of family dysfunction, alcoholism, and grief, spoke about the effect of other authors' writings on him and his desire to, in turn, strongly affect his readers. When asked by *The Rumpus* why he wrote about his life, he responded, "Before I had my writing, I had other people's writing. I had poems and essays and stories from men and women who had lost their fathers long before I did, and who had fallen in love, and then, out of it. I had the words of people who had suffered and struggled, who felt small and invisible, who felt ugly, who admitted strange and taboo things in book pages and stood bravely behind their humanness and managed to

Creativity Booster
Making the Personal Universal

Many Sensitive Souls write memoirs, semi-autobiographical novels, plays, screenplays, or poems to help them understand their own lives and experiences and inspire others who are searching for meaning about *their* lives. Avoid the common error of thinking the more details you provide about your life, the harder it will be for your audience to relate. Ironically, the opposite is true. The audience will take your experiences and find parallels in their own lives. So, go ahead and describe your childhood home in the Sonoran Desert in Arizona, for instance, including sensory descriptions of the iguanas cross-ing your front walk and the prickly pear blossoms emerging from the cacti, and, believe it or not, it will bring back mem-ories for readers from coastal Maine and downtown Omaha.

keep going. I remember reading those words on city buses and in empty libraries, and I guess the hope is that I could add to it, pay it forward in some way and make some other kid on some city bus feel a little less alone."

Cautionary Tales for the Sensitive Soul

It's not always easy being a Sensitive Soul. The very qualities that make you a great artist—empathy and insight—may also feel like a burden at times. Let's look at some of the challenges you might face and those tendencies you can tame in order to make meaningful art while also being a wee bit self-protective.

Creativity Booster
Naming Your Fears

Sensitive Souls tend to produce creative work stemming from difficult, painful life experiences. No wonder you feel afraid of doing it sometimes! The first step toward overcoming, or at least making peace with, your fears is identifying them. Some fears common to Sensitive Souls are:

- Feeling unsure if anyone else will relate to your life
- Being judged for exposing family secrets
- Finding it painful to delve into difficult personal experiences
- Not being able to "save" anybody with your work
- Worrying that a diagnosis of a mood disorder— or the drugs to treat it—might diminish your creativity rather than contribute to it

See which of these resonate with you, and add three more of your own fears to the list. Then, answer the question "What can I do?" for each one. For instance, if your worst fear is that certain family members will attack you if you expose your family's dark side, think about what you could do to either tolerate their judgment and/or denial or mitigate some of the bad feelings, possibly before you release your work to the world. Repeat this exercise with your other fears, and see if it lessens the intensity of each one.

Mood Disorders and Creativity

You might be someone who has to cope with a mood disorder. If so, know that you are in the company of many of history's most celebrated artists.

The stereotype of the "suffering artist" has gained acceptance because many famous artists really have led anguished lives. In the past, it was thought they suffered because they were "oversensitive" or had a compulsion to live life on the edge of a knife. But, today, it's clear a lot of them likely had clinical mood disorders such as anxiety, depression, or bipolar disorder and, in some cases, schizophrenia.

Sylvia Plath was one such writer. And, yet, we shouldn't allow her depression and suicide to define the whole of her life. When I read her journals, it came as a surprise to learn how much hope and optimism she'd felt even after she'd already experienced episodes of severe depression and had attempted suicide. Her love of writing and·specific ambitions sustained her and propelled her forward. In one entry she explains, "I want to write because I have the urge to excel in one medium of translation and expression of life. I can't be satisfied with the colossal job of merely living."

Another famous writer, William Styron, came out about being afflicted with paralyzing depression before people talked so openly about mood disorders. He did so in his 1990 memoir, *Darkness Visible: A Memoir of Madness*, and also in a piece he wrote for *Vanity Fair*, detailing the horrors of sinking lower and lower into that "darkness." But, he also acknowledged how depression has fueled masterpieces in all arenas of art, writing, "Through the course of literature and art the theme of depression has run like a durable thread of woe," citing, among other artistic works, Hamlet's soliloquy, Emily Dickinson's verses, Nathaniel Hawthorne's and Edgar Allan Poe's fiction, Albrecht Dürer's engravings, Van Gogh's "manic wheeling stars," Beethoven's symphonies, and Bach's cantatas.

This link between mood disorders and creativity is no longer simply a matter of personal testimony or observation by others. It's become a subject for researchers, too.

A 2008 study conducted by psychiatrist Nancy Andreasen and published in *Dialogues in Clinical Neuroscience* centered on students and professors at the famed Iowa Writers' Workshop. While the majority of writers in the study had significant histories of mood disorders and most had received treatment, Andreasen discovered they tended to experience relatively brief periods of high or low moods lasting weeks to months, interspersed with long periods of "normal" moods. When Andreasen met with the writers, they all appeared upbeat and entertaining and seemed to be living interesting, satisfying lives. In other words, they didn't fit the stereotype of the tortured artist despite their condition.

She found that they, and creative people generally, have some distinctive qualities that make life both richer and perhaps more difficult. They tend to be vulnerable, open to new experiences, and comfortable with ambiguity. They live a life that isn't based on preconceptions or authoritarian rules. Their inner worlds are complex and comprise more shades of gray than those of people living "regular" lives. Does this describe you?

As she also noted, creative people often have to contend with criticism or rejection or being treated as odd, and that can lead to feelings of depression or social alienation. So, it makes sense that there's a two-way street running between mood disorders and creativity.

The Creative Sweet Spot

Psychologist Kay Redfield Jamison, author of *Touched with Fire: Manic-Depressive Illness and the Artistic Temperament*, has also noted an association between creativity and mood disorders. Jamison contends that severe mania or depression can prevent an artist from being fully productive. Extreme mania would make it hard for someone to settle down and focus in or edit, while extreme depression would sap someone of the necessary energy and desire to create. But those suffering from hypomania (mild mania) or melancholy (mild depression) or alternating between the two might be in the sweet spot for creativity. According to Jamison, people in a mildly manic state think more quickly, fluidly, and originally, while those in a melancholic state are self-critical and obsessive, which is perfect for doing work like revisions and editing. Melancholy may also allow people to recall painful times—but at a safe distance—and enable them to tap into deeper emotions and their unconscious and sharpen their perspective.

Jamison is not diminishing the seriousness of even these milder states, but she believes the interplay between hypomania and melancholy may supply a fertile ground for creativity. She writes, "There's something about the experience of prolonged periods of melancholia—broken at times by episodes of manic intensity and expansiveness—that leads to a different kind of insight, compassion, and expression of the human condition."

The Emotional Risks of Creating

One of the significant side effects of creativity—but one for which there is a variety of antidotes—is the emotional difficulty of delving into painful memories, feelings, or revelations.

Tackling the past presents a serious conundrum if you're a Sensitive Soul: on the one hand, exploring painful emotions like grief or sorrow can be cathartic and help you make some sense of traumas. On the other hand, doing so keeps you steeped in upsetting and painful issues and emotions. It can be tempting to give up, procrastinate, avoid going "there," or make light of subjects requiring deep digging.

This is a struggle I've noticed in my writing workshops: sometimes a student will drop a one-line hint about a traumatizing experience that may not even be related to the rest of his or her essay. That's a signal to me that they really do want to write about this event but might not be ready to take it on yet. If you find yourself in this position, it's okay—you shouldn't force yourself to deal with a heavy subject you're not ready to address. But, be aware that if you're dipping your toe in the water, it may mean you're more ready to immerse yourself than you realize. I hope you'll dive in if you feel up to it. Of course, there is the risk of getting in over your head.

Musician Sufjan Stevens struggled with this dilemma. When he lost his mother at a young age, his grief was complicated by the fact that she had left the family when Stevens was one and had never established a close relationship with him. So, how do you deal with the loss of the mother you never really had?

In Stevens's case, he recorded an album, *Carrie and Lowell*, named for his mother and stepfather, that delves into his confusion and despair. Writer Dave Eggers, who is no stranger to suffering himself, having lost both his parents at a young age, called it a "brutal, extremely sad, relentlessly wrenching record."

In an interview with Eggers, Stevens said, "I was recording songs as a means of grieving, making sense of it. But the writing and recording wasn't the salve I expected. I fell deeper and deeper into doubt and misery. It was a year of real darkness." And, so, the experience of making the album wasn't what he had hoped; it didn't bring him the emotional relief he was seeking. But, it did allow him to relinquish some anger and, it seems, to reach a place of some forgiveness for the mother who had not mothered him. And, of course, Stevens can also take comfort in knowing the result of his painful process helps console listeners who've been through similar experiences.

Spotlight: Janis Joplin, Feeling Everyone's Pain

Poet Robert Lowell captured the difficulty of being a Sensitive Soul, saying it was a matter of "seeing too much and feeling it with one skin-layer missing." Not only are Sensitive Souls vulnerable, but also they are attuned to other people's feelings, including their pain, and they experience it with almost the same intensity as the other person. Needless to say, this can make for a tough life—and raw and searing art.

If any artist fits this description, it's the singer **Janis Joplin**. The phrase "gut-wrenching" could have been invented to describe Joplin's singing. Listen to "Summertime" or "Cry Baby," and your gut will be wrenched for sure.

Joplin grew up in the 1940s and 1950s in Port Arthur, Texas, a bastion of conformity, and suffered what Virginia Woolf in *A Room of One's Own* called "contrary instincts." Joplin fervently wanted to fit in, but she knew she not only could never fit in but to try would crush her soul.

A decade after Joplin graduated from high school and became one of the biggest rock stars of the 1960s, she returned for her class's ten-year reunion, cutting a resplendent figure with her tinted granny glasses and feathers in her hair. When she was asked by an interviewer if she'd gone to her high school prom, she responded that she hadn't been asked and feigned hysteria at the rejection. But, in truth, the rejection and the bullying about her so-called unfeminine looks and facial acne had stung her so badly she still carried the hurt. Years later, Ellen Willis, a music critic for *Rolling Stone*, wrote that Joplin had "suffered the worst fate that can befall an adolescent girl in America—*unpopularity.*"

Around the time of her visit home, Joplin's boyfriend broke up with her because she couldn't kick her heroin habit, an addiction that killed her at age twenty-seven. On the road, she found herself alone in her hotel room at night while the guys in the band slept around, and loneliness and despair crept in. In the PBS American Masters documentary *Janis: Little Girl Blue*, one of her bandmates commented that Joplin had been receiving the love of millions, but if one person didn't love her, it destroyed her.

As someone with Sensitive Soul qualities, Joplin wasn't only in touch with her own pain. In the same documentary, her ex said of her, "She could feel everybody's pain. One of the reasons she did heroin was so she didn't have to be involved with everybody else's life. Most people can be oblivious to what's going on around them, but Janis couldn't. She couldn't block it out."

Another bandmate, Dave Getz, teared up and his voice cracked as he thought back to the Janis he'd known, saying, "She was in touch with her own emotions, and who she was, in some way that nobody else I knew was. And, to be that way—to try to get that—that's the price you pay for doing that kind of art on that level."

Can Sensitive Souls avoid paying such a steep price? It's worth taking a look at artists with strong emotional resonance like Meryl Streep and Adele, who choose to live seemingly unglamorous daily lives, away from Hollywood and other celebrity haunts. They come across as grounded yet simultaneously free to do their work without it taking a permanent toll on them or destroying them. Perhaps a protective layer of self-preservation through "normalcy" can help ground the Sensitive Soul.

Recording Life's Moments, Large and Small

Some Sensitive Souls attempt to record every moment of life—or at least every special one—so that none is forgotten or lost. Their smartphone is really more of a camera and journal than a phone to them, and they capture people, places, and experiences in a frantic effort to guard against loss, even though they know loss is inevitable. If this is something you do, it's worth asking yourself, is my obsession with holding onto life causing me to, ironically, miss out on life?

Sarah Manguso captures this compulsion in her book *Ongoingness: The End of a Diary*. In twenty-five years, she'd written an astounding 800,000 words in her diary, recording as many moments as possible. As she describes this Herculean effort, "I wrote so I could say I was truly paying attention. Experience in itself wasn't enough. The diary was my defense against waking up at the end of my life and realizing I'd missed it."

But, Manguso also came to understand that as much as she'd journaled on a daily basis, so much more was lost to oblivion. And, also, there was so much she'd missed out on by paying attention only to the beginning and ending of an experience or relationship rather than the middle, the meat, of it.

Elizabeth Alexander, poet and author of the memoir *The Light of the World* about the sudden death of her beloved husband, Ficre, at the age of fifty, has also wrestled with the artist's attachment to memories and remembering. In *Light*, she asks, "How much space for remembering is there in a day? How much should there be? I think about this in my poetry. I don't want to be a nostalgist. Yet I feed on memory, I need it to make poems, the art that is made of the stuff I have: my life and the world around me." She also acknowledges, "I write to fix him in place, to pass time in his company, to make sure I remember, even though I know I will never forget."

After struggling with the all-too-human temptation to hold on tightly to life, experiences, and people, both of these authors seemed to arrive at some understanding of how to infuse their art with memories without letting those memories completely overwhelm their lives. And you, Sensitive Soul, will surely learn to do the same.

The Takeaway

If you're a Sensitive Soul or someone with Sensitive Soul tendencies, you're full of feelings you get to pour into your creative projects. You don't just have a desire to create; you have an urgent need to do so.

What can you do to make the most of your temperament while not allowing emotions to cloud your artistic judgment or succumbing to the dangerous mythology of the "tortured artist"?

- Be proud of your sensitivity and depth of feelings; they will benefit you, creatively.
- See if doing art can bring you some catharsis or greater understanding of your life.
- Remember that creativity also springs from happiness and joy, not just despair.
- Realize that sometimes you need some distance between you and an experience you want to capture.
- When you're feeling lonely, find ways to connect with people through doing art.
- If you're feeling isolated, escape into your imagination.
- Use your artistic talents to make a difference in the life of another person.
- Don't just record life. Live it!

Chapter 5

THE ACTIVIST: CHANGING THE WORLD THROUGH ART

ᘐᘛ

Poets are the unacknowledged legislators of the world.

—Percy Bysshe Shelley, "A Defence of Poetry"

Do you believe art can change the world? Stop wars, free the oppressed, end poverty?

Maybe you miss the 1960s (even if you weren't alive then). Or, you go to Indigo Girls concerts wearing your Bob Marley T-shirt and John Lennon specs so all your peacenik idols can be represented in one place at the same time.

You realize the songs "Born This Way" or "Same Love" didn't directly lead to the Supreme Court's ruling in favor of same-sex marriage. But, you're pretty sure that when Justice Anthony Kennedy was writing the majority opinion, he was lip syncing those songs while binge-watching old episodes of *Glee* and reading David Sedaris's essays in *Me Talk Pretty One Day*. Your greatest wish is to compose a song or produce a TV show or write an essay collection with *that* kind of impact, one that has the potential to change the course of people's lives or even the course of history.

You just might be an Activist.

Why Do Activists Create?

If you're an Activist or have Activist tendencies, you tend to see injustices everywhere you look, and you can't stand idly by. You have to *do* something about it—you have no choice. Here are the likely reasons why you create.

Because every time you see that damned public service ad with the sad-eyed dogs and the haunting song playing in the background, it slays you. Because you really *can* imagine a world with no countries and no religion, too. Because you can't be satisfied writing neo-noir thrillers or photographing celebrities for magazine covers or playing the star's BFF in a rom-com—not when your talents could be put to a higher purpose.

Because you're a political news junkie, but you're first and foremost a writer or dancer or painter. Because you can remember reading *To Kill a Mockingbird* and comprehending, for the first time, how a novel could make you not just intellectually understand big issues like injustice but actually feel them in your bones. Because you want to matter, and you want your art to matter.

Snapshot of an Activist

Activists are especially driven because, on any given day, there are so many wrongs that need righting. If you're an Activist, you'll never run out of material to inspire you.

You don't just have a desire to use your creativity for a political purpose—you feel a sense of duty to do so.

There's often an *urgency* to your work. When it comes to performing a slam poem about police shootings of unarmed black men or doing street art with an antiwar message, time is of the essence.

Activists are often accused of being naive idealists, and most of them accept that as a compliment (even when it's not intended as

Artistic Personality Quiz
So, You Think You're an Activist

1. Do you see wrongs that need righting everywhere you look? Will you be unable to live with yourself unless you respond in some fashion?
2. Are you interested in politics but would rather use your creative talents than a law degree or public office to make a change?
3. Do you imagine a time when there are no more wars, no poverty, no violence against women—when everyone can just get along?
4. Do you think writing love songs, nighttime soaps, or action-adventure movies is fine, but you see yourself as doing art that's grander, that could improve the sorry state of the world?
5. Do you believe artists have a *duty* to use their artistic talents for political purpose?
6. Are you concerned with finding a balance between artistry and a political message (without sacrificing one for the other)?
7. Do you take pride in being politically incorrect in your art?
8. Do you sometimes feel you've been selected, against your will, to represent "your people" through your work?
9. Do you not just talk the talk (in your art) but also walk the walk (in your life) when it comes to issues you're passionate about?
10. Are you willing to risk the type of backlash artists throughout history have endured for the sake of making political art?

If you answered "yes" to most of these questions, you are an Activist. And, if you answered "yes" to even a few of these questions, you have strong Activist tendencies. Either way, read on.

one). Their thinking goes, if you don't dream big about the power of art and the power of political action, how can you ever expect to make the world a better place?

As an Activist, you believe art can change minds and reach into the heart of someone's heart.

You may have already wrestled with quandaries unique to Activists. Can you prevent your work from becoming too message-heavy? Is art with political purpose as effective in achieving change as direct action, rallies, or politics?

Since Activists throughout the world speak truth to power, there's a real possibility those in power may fight back and even place Activist artists in jail or exile them if that's what it takes to silence them.

But Activists won't be silenced. Your art will find its way out into the world.

Varieties of Activists

You might be the sort of Activist who wants your art to have shock value. Or, you might be the kind of Activist who is intent on achieving a balance of message and artistry.

See the Sidebar for a list of varieties of Activists, and read on for an exploration of some of the most common ones.

The Advocate

Advocating for a cause is the lifeblood of an Activist. For many Activists, doing message-driven art is not so much a choice as it is a necessity, considering the state of the world.

In "Why I Write," George Orwell admits that, given his druthers, he would have preferred to write purely for the joy of writing.

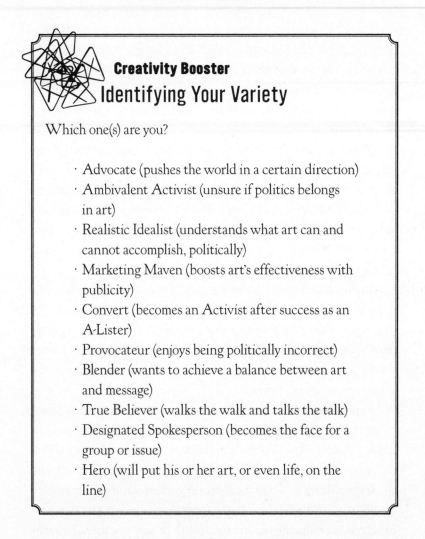

Creativity Booster

Identifying Your Variety

Which one(s) are you?

- Advocate (pushes the world in a certain direction)
- Ambivalent Activist (unsure if politics belongs in art)
- Realistic Idealist (understands what art can and cannot accomplish, politically)
- Marketing Maven (boosts art's effectiveness with publicity)
- Convert (becomes an Activist after success as an A-Lister)
- Provocateur (enjoys being politically incorrect)
- Blender (wants to achieve a balance between art and message)
- True Believer (walks the walk and talks the talk)
- Designated Spokesperson (becomes the face for a group or issue)
- Hero (will put his or her art, or even life, on the line)

In other words, he was most likely an Artisan at heart. But, instead, because of the tumultuous times he'd lived through—both world wars, the rise of Fascism and Nazism, the mass murder of millions of people—he felt he had a *duty* to try to change the world through his writing, and so "political purpose" became his primary motive for writing.

He felt *compelled* to write with an activist aim, going so far as to claim, "Every line of serious work that I have written since 1936 has been written, directly or indirectly, *against* totalitarianism and *for* democratic socialism, as I understand it. It seems to me nonsense, in a period like our own, to think that one can avoid writing of such subjects."

Although she was born decades later, writer Barbara Kingsolver would have made the perfect high tea companion for Orwell since her views on politics in literature overlap so much with his own. In her case, it was the prevailing attitudes about the Gulf War (1990–1991) that got under her skin, especially when a man who walked by her at an antiwar rally told her to "love it or leave it," meaning the United States. She left.

In the grand tradition of literary expatriates before her, like F. Scott Fitzgerald and James Baldwin, she moved to Europe, in part to see if she could write about her country with greater clarity from a distance. While living in Spain, she wrote an essay, "Jabberwocky," in which she took on a litany of wrongs occurring in the United States at the time.

Kingsolver believes creators have a duty to society, writing, "The artist's maverick responsibility is sometimes to sugarcoat the bitter pill and slip it down our gullet, telling us what we didn't think we wanted to know." The bitter pill is the political truth, and the sugarcoating is the artistic delivery. According to Kingsolver, novels like *Beloved* or *Jane Eyre* can accomplish what a news report cannot by introducing readers to difficult or ugly situations like slavery, war, or women's oppression and making such readers really *feel* for these characters. When people have empathy for others, even fictional others, they soften their stance and are no longer so willing to go to war or pit one group against another. And, so, Kingsolver considers the fiction writer's talent at instilling empathy in his or her readers a subtle—and subtly effective—form of advocacy.

Creativity Booster
Choosing an Issue

You're someone who's passionate about all sorts of issues, and sometimes you feel moved to design an art installation, compose a song, or perform a spoken word poem to express your infuriation with societal wrongs. That's awesome. But, you might want to narrow your focus to those issues where you could have the greatest potential impact. What do you consider the wrong you most want to see righted? What's an issue that's ripe for change? What's not being talked about that should be? Is there one particular cause you most want to become associated with, one you might devote yourself to, year after year? See if answering these questions leads you to making the right choices for you.

Fiction also provides a space for authors to advocate for their philosophical views, as Ayn Rand did with Objectivism in her opus *Atlas Shrugged*. The novel's plot centers around a dystopian United States in which the most creative industrialists, scientists, and artists go on strike against the so-called welfare state and retreat to a mountainous hideaway where they build an independent free economy. Rand's beliefs come through loud and clear: the proper moral purpose of one's life is the pursuit of one's own happiness, and the only worthwhile social system is laissez-faire capitalism. Libertarians and conservatives have drawn inspiration from this philosophy ever since the novel, Rand's last, was published in 1957 to mostly negative reviews but strong and enduring popularity.

The Ambivalent Activist

Not all artists are comfortable with injecting political purpose into their art. Some believe art should be pure, untainted, and apolitical, with no motive other than to move and entertain an audience— make them think, feel, cry, laugh. And, it certainly shouldn't in-volve imposing your viewpoint on your audience. Leave that to politicians and pundits, not artists!

As an Activist, you may already be struggling with the con-flict between "pure" art and political art. You wonder, does *all* your work need to contain a message? Will you offend your fans if you get *too* political? Maybe you're worried publishers or record labels won't be interested in you, your sales will decline, or you'll get a reputation. You're committed to making art with political purpose, but you aren't sure you want to feel like you *have* to.

All of these concerns are legit, and lots of artists—aspiring or famous—have grappled with them. I once attended a panel discus-sion at my hometown library in Newton, Massachusetts, about why writers write. During the Q&As, an audience member who's writing a novel asked the panelists for advice. He wanted so much for his book to contain a meaningful message but felt overwhelmed by this goal, and as a result, he was stuck. One of the panelists, Andre Dubus III, gave him a simple and simply stated piece of ad-vice: "Try not to say a thing. Just try to capture the truth, bro." In other words, allow your message to flow through naturally rather than forcing it.

Francine Prose captured the difficulty she and other writers experience in trying to reconcile artistry with activism. As she put it in an essay in *The New York Times*, "So what's a writer to do? We want to write the loveliest, truest, most original and affecting sen-tence, the most musical poetic line. But meanwhile we may notice that the world is going to hell in a hand basket; and there we are, in our comfy ergonomic desk chairs, pursuing an activity that, we fear, is less socially useful than cultivating hydrangeas." Her potential solution? "To separate our responsibility as artists (to art) from our human responsibility (to other human beings)." In other words, to stay "pure" in art while engaging in political issues in life.

Another writer who tried to separate his art from his activism was the twentieth-century British poet W. H. Auden. There's no doubt Auden felt a sense of duty to politics: he went to Spain to join the fight against the Fascist dictator Francisco Franco. Afterwards, he gave speeches against Fascism and even wrote a pamphlet-length poem, "Spain," with proceeds going to an international organization supporting the anti-Franco cause. But he would eventually renounce and try to suppress the poem, embarrassed by what he considered its childish politics and poor verse.

Following those experiences, Auden started to question the effectiveness of politically driven art. When he wrote the poem "In Memory of W. B. Yeats" in honor of his literary idol, he included this controversial line: "Poetry makes nothing happen." For decades, critics have pored over these four words, trying to figure out why in the world a poet—especially one of Auden's standing—would make such a discouraging claim.

Why was Auden, who was famous in his own time, a time when socially conscious writers and poets were held in such high esteem, so repelled by mixing activism with art?

He seemed to fear that adding political language and meaning to his poetry would sully it. Auden, after all, wrote some of the most gorgeous love poetry ever. If you want, watch the eulogy scene in the movie Four Weddings and a Funeral for a sob-inducing reading of one of his most beloved poems, "Funeral Blues (Stop All the Clocks)." Maybe Auden just plain didn't want to feel pressured into doing things a certain way to appease other politically minded artists and writers.

Neither does Thom Yorke, the frontman for the alternative rock band Radiohead. In 2003, the band released the album *Hail to the Thief*, an obvious play on "hail to the chief"—with the thief/chief being President George W. Bush, whose claims that Saddam Hussein was hiding weapons of mass destruction supplied the rationale for invading Iraq. It would be tough to deny this album name has political connotations, right? And yet, when asked, Yorke insisted the band was not directly political, at least not intentionally.

Really? Because much as the album title might have been a lark, it sure sounds political. Yet Yorke told *Resonance Magazine*, "I don't think there is much that's genuinely political art that is good art. The first requirement is that it's good art, and if it is, then there's a sense of escape." One of Yorke's chief criticisms is that "the language of politics is ugly" and "definitely not a thing of beauty."

But not everyone agrees. Magical realism writer Italo Calvino saw an opportunity to use beautiful language to convey political or social views. As he states in *The Uses of Literature*, he believes political literature is best when it "gives a voice to whatever is without a voice, when it gives a name to what as yet has no name, especially to what the language of politics excludes or attempts to exclude." And, in a more lyrical style, Calvino writes: "Literature is like an ear that can hear things beyond the understanding of the language of politics; it is like an eye that can see beyond the color spectrum perceived by politics."

Alice Walker, who's been instrumental in both the civil rights and women's movements, used to worry that "being an activist and writing about it 'demoted' [her] to the level of 'mere journalism.'" Then she had a realization that sums up the pro-political purpose viewpoint for both journalists and artists. She writes in *Anything We Love Can Be Saved*, "Now I know that, as with the best journalists, activism is often my muse."

If activism is also your muse, pay attention. Remember, no muse wants to be ignored! So, be conscious of the debate about the role of political messaging in art, but go with your gut on this. Do work you're driven to do. Later in this chapter you'll find suggestions on how to blend art and politics.

The Realistic Idealist

As an Activist, one of your most admirable—and endearing— qualities is your idealism. You do what you do because you're sad-dened or appalled by or even self-righteously indignant about the state of the world, the world we're going to leave to our children, to future generations. And you fervently believe art can make a difference.

And, yet, sometimes it's hard, even for a hardcore Activist, to keep from questioning, as Auden did, whether art with political purpose can succeed in inciting change. And it's even harder to ignore some of the proclamations other famous writers and artists have made on this subject.

Take V. S. Naipaul, who, in his acceptance speech for the 2001 Nobel Prize for Literature, declared that "fiction is dead" and only nonfiction could address the complexities of our world. (And then he went on to write several more novels.)

In the 1990s, satirical author Don DeLillo liked to claim that the terrorist had supplanted the novelist in cultural relevance. "Not long ago, a novelist could believe he could have an effect on our consciousness of terror," he told *The New York Times*. "Today, the men who shape and influence human consciousness are the terror-ists." (And then he went on to write more novels.)

Jonathan Franzen also fretted about the relevance of the message-driven novel in his essay "Why Bother?," noting the world is changing so fast, other forms of art and the news are better at dealing with social issues than the novel. (And then he went on to write more novels.)

You may have noticed that while these novelists have done quite a bit of hand-wringing over the relevance—or lack thereof—of socially conscious novels, they continued to write them anyway. Remember, sweeping declarations like theirs are irresistible to make and hard to stand by. It's clear that, despite their fear of the dwindling influence of the novel, they still believe—they *must* believe—in its power.

As an Activist, you, too, believe art has great influence. And, yet, one of the toughest realities an Activist must face is the tortoise-slow pace of political and social change. You might fantasize that you'll write and perform an antiwar song that will go viral, be heard by millions around the globe, inspire marches and protests, and get the president of the United States to, for instance, withdraw all troops immediately from the Middle East.

Sorry, but that last part isn't going to happen. Not because of a song.

It hurts my heart when I see the crestfallen looks on my students' faces after I make them aware that Bob Dylan released the antiwar songs "Blowin' in the Wind" and "Masters of War" in 1963, but the United States did not leave Vietnam until *a full decade later.*

How can an Activist keep the faith when there's so much cause for resignation and so little basis for optimism? How do you stay motivated when it can be difficult to measure the effect of political art?

You, dear Activist, can become what I'm calling a realistic idealist—someone who holds onto their ideals but is also realistic about what art can and cannot accomplish. You can also take comfort in the knowledge that many socially conscious works of art throughout the centuries have made a demonstrable difference in social policies or in individuals' lives—sometimes it just takes time.

Listen to historian Howard Zinn, an exemplary realistic idealist. As Zinn said in *Resonance Magazine*, "Art may not be a blunt
instrument, but it will have a kind of poetic effect." He described
being in South Africa during apartheid in the early 1980s and
going to the Market Theater in Johannesburg to see plays featuring both black and white actors, a radical choice at the time. Zinn
understood a single play wasn't going to end apartheid but that "art
work[s] slowly over a period of time like wind and water eroding
rock." This is true even in the digital and social media era. Art
can change the world, but the process is more evolutionary than
revolutionary.

Spotlight: Artists Who've Made a Demonstrable Difference

Activist, if you ever lose faith in art's power to foster change,
here are some examples of artists and the work they did that made
a difference.

The Exonerated is an award-winning play by **Erik Jensen and
Jessica Blank** telling the true stories of six wrongfully convicted
death row inmates. In December 2002, a star-studded cast, including Richard Dreyfus, Danny Glover, and Mike Farrell, performed
the play to an audience that included Illinois governor George
Ryan. Ryan was in the midst of deciding the fate of death row inmates, and a month after seeing the play he commuted all 167 Illinois death sentences to prison terms of life or less shortly before
completing his term in office.

Herbert Block, an American political cartoonist, drew several
cartoons warning of the dangers of the United States becoming iso-
lationist and not joining the Allies in World War II. One, captioned
"Is this what you mean?," depicts a man showing a map of the world

to another man holding up a sign with a single word: "Isolation." On the map, most of the world's countries are painted black and display the German, Japanese, and Russian flags. He and other political cartoonists are believed to have played a role in swaying public opinion in favor of the United States entering World War II.

Conversely, during the Vietnam War, as antiwar sentiment grew from a countercultural movement to a more mainstream one, photographs of the horrors of war in the pages or even on the covers of popular magazines sped the process of withdrawing troops from Vietnam. If you were around in the 1960s, you surely remember the now-iconic, Pulitzer Prize–winning one by AP photographer **Nick Ut** of naked children running down the street, terrified, away from where a napalm bomb had mistakenly been set off by the South Vietnamese military against its own citizens. In another horrifying image, the chief of the South Vietnamese National Police, Nguyen Ngoc Loan, was captured in the moment of executing at point-blank range a member of the National Liberation Front, Nguyen Van Lem. This photograph by photojournalist **Eddie Adams** is credited with possibly doing more damage to the war effort than any video footage or print piece.

The Marketing Maven

Another aspect of being a realistic idealist is recognizing when making political art might not be enough to accomplish your goals. Sometimes a little marketing savvy can go a long way toward influencing behavior (registering people to vote, protesting fracking) or changing laws (such as those regulating guns).

Sound too "strategic" and not "artistic" enough? Well, you might be surprised at some of the artists who've subscribed to this approach—John Lennon, for one.

Lennon comes across as an art purist. After all, what's more idealistic than his timeless and universal song "Imagine"? What's more optimistic than "Give Peace a Chance" and "Happy Xmas (War Is Over)," both antiwar songs with an upbeat message? But Lennon didn't rely on his music alone to carry his message. Why not?

He was familiar with Bob Dylan's protest songs and understood how they had helped spark the antiwar movement but hadn't accomplished their larger aims of ending U.S. involvement in Vietnam.

And, so, in 1969, during the height of the war, Lennon and his much-maligned wife, avant-garde artist Yoko Ono, invited the global press to spend their honeymoon with them at the Amsterdam Hotel, where they started their Bed-Ins for Peace. That's right—they literally spent the day in PJs in bed, with the media surrounding them.

They also launched a massive public service campaign. Billboards in New York, London, Hollywood, Toronto, Paris, Rome, Berlin, Athens, and Tokyo proclaimed "War Is Over!" in giant black letters on a white background, with "If You Want It" in medium letters beneath it, and then, in smaller type at the bottom, "Happy Christmas from John and Yoko." The provocative message was also printed on posters and leaflets and in large spreads in major newspapers.

Lennon undoubtedly wished his songs alone would have been enough to sway people, but he understood the power of tag-teaming them with promotional tools. As he said, "Now I understand what you have to do: Put your political message across with a little honey."

The Internet and social media have made the one-two punch of art and messaging more potent than ever. In January 2016, a mural by the street artist Banksy appeared in London on a wall opposite the French embassy. It's a reimagining of the iconic image of

Cosette from the musical *Les Misérables*, crying as a cloud of tear gas envelopes her.

The image is a sharp critique of the use of tear gas by French police in the Calais refugee camp, where approximately five thousand people from countries like Syria and Libya had settled. The police denied using tear gas, but a video surfaced that showed otherwise. Banksy surpassed his standard use of stenciled art and turned the Cosette mural into his first interactive work. Beneath the image, he stenciled a QR barcode passersby could scan with their smartphones so they could view the shocking footage online.

Banksy was once asked by *The New Yorker* what drew him to street art. "I used to want to save the world," he wryly answered, "but now I'm not sure I like it enough." Clever response, but he obviously likes it enough to keep trying to fix it. As Rachel Campbell Johnston, the *London Times* art critic, told *The Daily Beast*, "All art is political in some way, but Banksy always has that quick response." She added, "He uses art as a weapon." You, too, could use art as a weapon.

The Convert

Many artists remain one creative type throughout their lives, propelled by the same drives they've had since childhood. But for some artists, their creative type changes as *they* change and their worldview expands or their goals are transformed. From what I've observed, the most common shift from one creative type to another is from A-Lister to Activist.

And this makes sense. In the beginning of their careers, a lot of artists are focused on getting noticed, making a name for themselves, and pursuing a commercial course. Once they've had some success, they begin to look outward and consider how they could use their art or their platform to make a difference in the world.

Creativity Booster
Enhancing Your Art's Impact

As an Activist, you're not content with people merely appreciating the beauty of your rhymes or paint strokes. You want to make people aware of an urgent problem, reconsider their perspective, or even take action. What can you do to reinforce the message of your art? You could design a social media campaign around the cause. You might partner with a nonprofit organization with similar concerns. For a local issue, you might plaster posters of your political art all around town. If doing publicity feels uncomfortable to you at first, remember that it's not to promote yourself, it's to promote an issue you care deeply about.

French "photograffeur" and street artist JR didn't start out as an Activist, but he sure became one. His early work consisted of tagging and doing other forms of street art on buildings around Paris as a means of proving *I am here, I exist*—an A-Lister attribute, to be sure.

But then, as he recalls in his memorable TED talk, he began to realize street art has real political possibilities and wondered, "Can art save the world?" In response, a friend chided him, "Maybe art can't save the world, but it can change the world." JR came to appreciate that art doesn't change the world directly but does touch people, and *they* then change the world. Those small doses of reality serum helped JR come to terms with the enormous—but not unlimited—potential of political art to have an impact.

Since then, he's traveled the globe, using his original photography and others' to make a difference in communities around the world, especially those hard hit by poverty, war, and mistreatment of women. He flyposts large black-and-white photographic images in public locations, calling the street "the largest art gallery in the world." For one project, JR took pictures of Israelis and Palestinians with identical jobs, such as nurse or cab driver, and posted enormous photos of them next to each other on both sides of the wall separating Israel from Palestine. Of course, the point was to pose a challenge to people without saying a word: can you tell who's Israeli and who's Palestinian? Aren't we more the same than we are different?

In another project, he plastered the roofs of homes in Kibera, Kenya, with dramatic photos of the eyes of the women in the village to honor them. He also printed the photos on vinyl rather than paper so that, for the first time, many of the residents had sturdy, leak-proof roofs. In all cases, JR's desire to change the world was his point of origin.

And, then there's a little-known singer named Beyoncé, a.k.a. Queen Bey. While there's been little debate about Beyoncé's immense talent, from her days as a teenager in Destiny's Child through her years as a solo artist, her girl power message has received a mixed response, with some women finding it empowering and others questioning whether her performances have been body positive or sexualized in a manner meant to attract and please men.

Then, in 2016, she performed her song "Formation" at the Super Bowl, which happens to take place during Black History Month, and followed up a few months later with the album *Lemonade* and its hour-long companion film. An Activist was born.

"Formation" is an unabashed black power anthem, evoking imagery of police brutality and the impact of Hurricane Katrina on African Americans. I think it's safe to say that nothing quite like it had been seen at the Super Bowl before. And, while *Lemonade* is a story of personal heartbreak and unfiltered rage over a real or fictional marital betrayal, and a fervid hope that love can endure, it is also a celebration of black women and "black girl magic." In one of the most affecting scenes, Beyoncé sits on a New Orleans police car slowly sinking underwater as images of blackness—mostly of female bodies and hair and faces—flash by. In this very Activist-by-way-of-A-Lister manner, Beyoncé used her superstar status not only to express her own beliefs but also to give voice to others in need of a voice, like abused or discounted women and mothers of unarmed African American boys and men killed by police officers.

If you're an Activist convert, don't feel like you have to fully abandon your A-Lister tendencies. JR and Beyoncé certainly haven't! Instead, if you take your desire for attention and refocus that attention on a cause you personally care about, imagine what you can achieve through art.

Positive Tendencies of Activists

Being Politically Incorrect

Being an Activist requires guts, and taking creative risks often involves crossing a line. But here's an interesting conundrum: the line is in a different place for everyone, so how can you even know if you're crossing it?

That is the question facing politically minded comedians who dare to tackle tough issues and subject themselves to all manner of response. Richard Pryor, Lenny Bruce, George Carlin, Roseanne, Bill Maher, Dave Chappelle, Sarah Silverman, Louis C.K., Amy Schumer—they've all, in their inimitable styles, stomped on the line, torn up the line, and even pushed the line so far out it's never moving back.

On an episode of *Inside the Actors Studio*, Dave Chappelle talks about the challenge of doing provocative comedy that is bound to upset people. He recalls how a viewer from Texas called Comedy Central "damned near 100 times," furious at him for the skit that served as what Chappelle refers to as his mission statement or manifesto for *Chappelle's Show*. The skit centers around the character Clayton Bigsby, a blind black man who believes he's white and—here's the brilliance of it—is a racist, shouting the N-word and other racial epithets and hanging around with white supremacists... until he discovers the truth.

Chappelle insists he wasn't mad at the caller for being mad at him. He acknowledges she might have even been right to criticize him but believes he has to call it as he sees it. Then he says something that seems to sum up the Activist's credo: "People that I love tell me I go too far sometimes. Maybe I went too far, but I did it... plus the only way you know where a line is is to cross it, and I think, what if nobody's crossing the line? You just want to try to be on the right side of history. Sometimes what's going on in the immediate present is not as important as the long term. The truth is permanent, and everything else falls by the wayside."

Amy Schumer has faced similar blowback for "going too far." After a parody of *Friday Night Lights* that skewered rape culture ran on her television show *Inside Amy Schumer*, she acknowledged at the Tribeca Film Festival that joking about rape is "always a risk." Schumer said, "You might look at this scene and think we're trying to make light of something serious, but really we are trying to educate."

Where's the line in your field of art? Do you push it out, even slightly, and risk the potential disapproval or even wrath of your readers or viewers and lots of Internet shaming? Yes you do. You're an Activist!

Fusing Politics and Art, or Yeah, You Blend

So, Activist, you want to bring politics into your art (or you wouldn't consider yourself the Activist type). I believe the central challenge for you is to "fuse political purpose and artistic purpose into one whole," as Orwell phrased it.

That's similar to how author Rick Moody describes his goal. He writes, "I have always tried to stake out political positions in what I do, but not in a manner, I hope, that is aesthetically dull... or too shrill, etc. I believe the two—aesthetics and politics—may go hand in hand."

But achieving such a balance is a challenge, and it often comes with certain sacrifices, like being more subtle than blatant, more "wink-wink" than direct, more mainstream than alternative. Not every artist wants to—or should—go this route. But if your goal is not just to promote your point of view but also to convince audience members to, at the very least, be open to more expansive ways of thinking, then you'll need to weigh these sacrifices against your larger goals.

And then there's the risk of becoming too message heavy. Most of us have seen a play or a movie and thought, "Uncle! Enough already. I *get* it!" That's a pretty good sign the Activist who wrote it was either content with preaching to the choir or didn't get the blend of art and politics quite right. You've got to trust your audience to understand subtext—the subtle message contained within the larger story.

Walking the Walk

If you're an Activist, you're not being asked to pass some moral purity test, but people do expect your life to encompass the values

Nurture Your Tendencies
Whip Up a Smooth Blend

Activist, I'd never want you to dull your fiery disposition. But if your goal is to fuse art and politics, here are a few questions you can ask yourself to make sure you're not getting too message heavy in your art: Is the character in my novel or play or TV show always speechifying instead of speaking? Have I added too many slogans or taglines to my collage for fear viewers won't otherwise get the point? Have I been editing my documentary to make the "good guy" seem perfect and the "bad guy" seem evil? Once you've answered these questions for yourself, you'll have a clearer sense of how to achieve your goals.

you espouse in your art. That's a pressure other creative types don't have to contend with. No one expected Pablo Picasso to be a feminist or Frank Lloyd Wright to be a nice, humble person. But, as an Activist, if you're going to sing songs about peace, you don't want to get caught on video punching someone out. If you're going to design an art installation with an environmental message, you really ought to recycle your bottles and cans!

For the most part, this is not a problem since Activists' art stems from their ardent beliefs. In fact, some Activists' artistry is so interconnected with their lives, there isn't much of a separation between the two. They not only indulge their political passions through their writing or art, they become directly involved with the causes they believe in. In other words, they walk the walk.

Sarah Kay is one such Activist. I first became aware of the power of spoken word poetry when one of my students showed a video in class of Kay performing her piece, "If I Should Have a Daughter." The language, the emotion, the passion of a future mother doing all she can to inspire and protect her daughter—it all came through. After the video went viral, Kay decided to found Project VOICE, an organization whose mission is to use spoken word poetry to "entertain, educate, and inspire." The members of Project VOICE visit schools, give performances, and hold workshops to help students build their confidence and craft their stories.

Another artist who walks the walk is playwright Eve Ensler, whose play *The Vagina Monologues*, along with her personal history as a survivor of sexual abuse, inspired her to start V-Day, an organization dedicated to eliminating violence against women. Every year, benefit productions of the play are held across the country, raising over $100 million as of this writing, which V-Day has used to help reopen women's shelters, produce public service announcements, and fund thousands of safe houses and antiviolence programs worldwide.

Ensler dismisses the line between art and activism, believing everything we do is political. She said on the Harvard Kennedy School PolicyCast, "If you choose to write a play that keeps people distracted from the issues at hand, that's a political decision. If you choose to write a play that engages people in the issues of our time, that's a political decision." Ensler's choice is clear, in her art and her life.

Cautionary Tales for the Activist

It's hard to keep a good Activist down. Your passion for a cause is a powerful impetus for doing creative work. Let's look at some of the challenges you might face and those tendencies you can tame in order to allow political purpose to guide, but not dictate, your art.

Creativity Booster
Naming Your Fears

Activists want to change the world, and they won't settle for anything less. Yet they know they could face a lot of blowback, and that can be pretty scary. The first step toward overcoming, or at least making peace with, your fears is identifying them. Some fears common to Activists are:

- Worrying that art may not be a powerful enough weapon for change
- Being expected by others to *always* do politically oriented art
- Allowing your message to overtake your artistry
- Losing your fan base because your stance is unpopular
- Subjecting yourself to possible censorship or backlash or even violence

See which of these resonate with you, and add three more of your fears to the list. Then, answer the question "What can I do?" for each one. For instance, if your worst fear is that you'll lose fans because you've taken an unpopular stance on an issue or in favor of a political candidate, realize that for each fan you lose, another one may appear. Or maybe you'll lose fans but experience the relief that comes from expressing yourself freely. Repeat this exercise with your other fears, and see if it lessens the intensity of each one.

The Designated Spokesperson

Say you become well known as an Activist, someone who isn't afraid to tackle the tough subjects—subjects others shy away from or pretend aren't problems. What do you do when you're then *expected* to always be political on behalf of a particular group or issue? That's what has happened to some artists, and it's a fate you might want to avoid.

James Baldwin wrote and spoke lyrically about his experience, and those of his characters, being black or gay or both in mid-twentieth-century America. He felt compelled to write about the struggles of people with these identities, and in fact his writings are considered a forerunner to the civil rights movement. But what was initially an individual, artistic choice became an expectation placed on him. Baldwin said in an interview, "Once I was in the civil-rights milieu, once I'd met Martin Luther King Jr. and Malcolm X and Medgar Evers and all those other people, the role I had to play was confirmed. I didn't think of myself as a public speaker, or as a spokesman, but I knew I could get a story past the editor's desk. And once you realize that you can do something, it would be difficult to live with yourself if you didn't do it." Even so, Baldwin resisted being labeled "the gay writer" or "the black writer." He just wanted people to think of him as a writer. Period.

A few decades later, filmmaker Spike Lee encountered the same problem as Baldwin did. I think his 1989 film *Do the Right Thing* is one of the best examples in any genre of blending the message with the medium. Issues of racism and economic injustice predominate, but Lee's characters are so lovable, so flawed, and so representative of New York's melting pot in all its glorious and messy complexity that the viewer walks away from the movie having seen many different perspectives.

Like Baldwin before him, Lee seeks artistic freedom, not demands. As he acknowledged in *The Atlantic Monthly*, "I'm always
being put in this position [where] I have to speak on race ... on behalf of 45 million African Americans." He doesn't want the pressure, the responsibility, or the restriction on his freedom.

It must be said that it's an honor to be the designated spokesperson for a cause. It shows you've made a real impression on
people and they look to you as a leader. But nothing destroys the
creative urge like feeling you're doing art out of obligation rather
than choice. So, should you find yourself in this position, even on a
smaller scale than Baldwin or Lee, be sure to insist on making the
art you want, not just the art others want you to make.

All in Due Time

Now and then an event is so unexpected and devastating, it defies
the usual rapid response by Activists. I'm thinking of the tragedy of
9/11, in particular, and how it seemed to leave everyone, including
Activists, reeling and wondering what to say, what to do. Most artists refrained from crafting a response in the immediate aftermath.

There were some notable exceptions: the Concert for New
York City was held on October 20, 2001, to raise money for char-
ity and to thank the first responders and honor those killed in the
attacks. Performers included Paul McCartney, the Who, Billy Joel,
Jerry Seinfeld, David Bowie, Elton John, and Adam Sandler as his
memorable character Opera Man. The live broadcast, lasting five
hours, raised over $35 million.

Another early effort was Bruce Springsteen's album, *The Ris-
ing*, released in July 2002. The *Asbury Park Press* posted this story
about Springsteen on its website: a few days after the attacks on the
World Trade Center, a man in a car stopped next to the rock god,

lowered his window and said, "We need you now." Springsteen figured the stranger was right and got to work.

Yet, there wasn't much commercial creative outpouring. In fact,
something like the opposite occurred. As you may remember, many
films and TV shows were postponed, altered, or even cancelled in
response to the attacks. The release dates for multiple movies were
postponed due to plot lines involving terrorism or other violent
acts. The start of the 2001–2002 television season was put on hold,
and season premieres originally slated for mid-September were
delayed until the end of the month. Some late-night talk shows remained off the air for days while the comedian-hosts tried to figure out an appropriate response. The Fifty-Third Primetime Emmy
Awards, originally scheduled for five days after 9/11, was delayed
by a few weeks and then another month to avoid coinciding with
the date the United States began a bombing campaign in Afghani-
stan. The list goes on.

Given the fraught atmosphere, it's not surprising Activists had
concerns about making films, songs, or plays about 9/11. Would
they appear too jingoistic or unpatriotic? Would they be perceived
as trying to capitalize on a tragedy? How could an artist address
a tragedy that represented so much geopolitical history and con-
flict? And, how could art come to terms with the attackers when
it wasn't even agreed upon whether they were madmen, religious
fanatics, an independent group of politicized men opposed to U.S.
foreign policy in the Middle East, or disciples of Osama bin Laden?

Most importantly, what was there to say and what was the
best art form for saying it? Eventually, despite their concerns, some
well-known authors—although not many—began writing novels
dealing directly or indirectly with 9/11, including *Saturday* by Ian
McEwan and *Extremely Loud and Incredibly Close* by Jonathan
Safran Foer (which was also made into a movie a decade after 9/11).

But, not everyone was satisfied. Laura Miller, book critic for *Salon*, wrote in 2011, a full decade after 9/11, that "even the best of these books can't seem to do more than circle around a void." Her explanation? "[The novel] is, in short, an engine for finding and generating meaning, which is why it is fundamentally at odds with the horrific interruption of that day: At its heart, 9/11 was meaningless." This could explain the difficulty filmmakers also faced.

Another challenge has also haunted writers and artists: how could art "compete" with the television news images of the towers going down—images that were repeated over and over and over again and burned into our collective memories?

When you feel overwhelmed by the enormity or so-called meaninglessness of an event, my advice to you is this: respond the way you feel compelled to, *when* you feel compelled to. Don't be daunted, don't be censored, but also don't feel rushed. Address the issues that mean the most to you and about which you have the most to say, and you'll know you did the right thing.

Putting Your Art—or Life—on the Line

Okay, Activist, it's time to get really real. As you've seen, artistic risk taking requires guts—and not only because you might offend or even lose some audience members. The global history of Activists, up to and including the present day, includes brave souls who have faced serious backlash, ranging from censorship to ruined reputations to lost income to incarceration, exile, beatings, and even death threats. Not to mention all the rude, racist, misogynist comments they—maybe you?—have been the target of on social media.

I don't mean to scare you away from Activist art. But, I think it's important to recognize you're part of an illustrious history of badass artists who put their work—or even their freedom or their very lives—on the line.

Here's a sampling of mostly twentieth-and twenty-first-century artists (and there are many more throughout the ages) who fought the good fight. Despite the risks and hardship, you'll see that there's often a silver lining: in many cases, their crucibles made these artists even more popular and successful than before.

Spotlight: Artists Willing to Risk It All

CENSORED, BANNED, OR BLACKLISTED

· In 1939, **Billie Holiday** recorded "Strange Fruit." The "fruit" is a metaphor for black people who'd been lynched and whose bodies were hanging from trees— a powerful and horrifying image, if ever there was one. Her record company, Columbia, would not allow her to record it in its studio but temporarily released her from her contract so she could put it out on a specialty label. While some U.S. radio stations refused to play it, others did, and the song sold one million copies in 1939, becoming Holiday's best-selling record. To enhance the drama of Holiday's performance of the song at the end of every set of hers at Café Society in Greenwich Village, the waiters stopped all service in advance, Holiday started off with her eyes closed as if she were lost in prayer, the room was kept dark except for a spotlight on Holiday's face, and no encores were allowed. "Strange Fruit" won multiple awards and recognition, including "Song of the Century" from *Time* magazine.

· In 1947, with American fear of Communism at its hysterical height, ten prominent directors and screenwriters had the courage to publicly denounce the tactics employed by the House Un-American Activities

Committee (HUAC), led by Senator Joseph McCarthy, during its probe of alleged Communist influence in Hollywood. All the members of this prominent group, dubbed the **"Hollywood Ten,"** were blacklisted—they received jail sentences and were banned from working for the major studios. In a satisfying twist, several movies were later made to honor the Hollywood Ten and remind audiences of this dark history, including *The Front*; *Good Night, and Good Luck*; and *Trumbo*.

· In 2003, during the Iraq War, **Dixie Chicks lead singer Natalie Maines** dissed President George W. Bush by telling a London concert audience that she was "ashamed the president of the United States is from Texas," the band members' home state. In response, Cumulus Broadcasting banned the Dixie Chicks' music from its 262 radio stations, the song "Travelin' Soldier" lost 15 percent of its airplay, and the band was toppled from its top spot on the Billboard country singles chart.

· In 2010, YouTube banned the music video for "Born Free" by female English rapper **M.I.A. (Mathangi Arulpragasam)**, citing violent content. M.I.A. made the video to protest the Sri Lankan Army's roundup and slaughter of Tamil men, a Sri Lankan ethnic group. But, here's one of those silver linings: YouTube's attempt at censorship appears to have boosted the popularity of the song and awareness of its political purpose.

CANCELLED

· No stranger to controversy, **Madonna** released the song and video for "Like a Prayer" in 1989. Although MTV played it, it also labeled it "controversial." Religious groups protested the burning of crosses in the video and the mix of sexual and religious imagery. As a result, Pepsi canceled a huge advertising contract it had with Madonna—but the pop singer got to keep the five-million-dollar payout. Pope John Paul II even weighed in, encouraging Catholics to boycott her performances. Naturally, these efforts backfired, and the video won the MTV Video Music Award for Viewer's Choice later that year.

· On September 17, 2001, less than a week after the 9/11 attacks, **Bill Maher**, on his aptly named show "Politically Incorrect," refuted President Bush's assertion that the terrorists were cowards, saying, "We have been the cowards, lobbing cruise missiles from 2,000 miles away. That's cowardly. Staying in the airplane when it hits the building, say what you want about it, [it's] not cowardly." In response, corporate sponsors including Sears and FedEx pulled their ads from the show. The following year, ABC decided not to renew its contract with Maher. Although the network denied its decision was related to the controversy, Maher and others didn't buy it.

ARRESTED, JAILED, OR BEATEN

· **Oscar Wilde**, the gay, Irish writer and poet perhaps best known for his play *The Importance of Being Earnest*, was imprisoned in 1895 for sodomy and gross indecency. Upon his release, broke and in poor health, he left England for Paris and gave up writing fairly soon afterward. "I can write but have lost the joy of writing," he said before dying in 1900.

· Between 1961 and 1964, comedian **Lenny Bruce** was arrested four times on obscenity charges. The first was after he used an insulting name involving the male anat' omy in his show at the Jazz Workshop in San Francisco. The second was for using the word "schmuck." His third and fourth arrests, both at the Café au Go Go in Greenwich Village in April 1964, happened after un' dercover agents alleged he used more than one hundred obscene words during a set. But in 2003, New York Governor George Pataki posthumously pardoned Bruce for those last two charges.

· Visual artist and Chinese dissident **Ai Weiwei** achieved international status when he spoke out against the 2008 Beijing Olympics after designing its centerpiece, and he has continued to criticize his government's abuses of democracy and human rights. One of his controversial works is a collection of photos called "Study of Perspec' tive," which shows him giving the finger to cultural and political power centers, including Tiananmen and the White House. In response to his outspoken views and brash art, he's been jailed and was allegedly so badly beaten by the police that he required brain surgery. He is also barred from leaving Beijing. In a TED film, Weiwei said, "I'm living in a society where freedom of speech is not allowed.... I'm trying to involve my art with society, to build possibility."

ESCAPED OR EXILED

· On January 13, 1898, French author **Émile Zola** risked his writing career and freedom when his "J'accuse" letter was published on the front page of the Paris daily, *L'Aurore*. The letter was aimed at French president Félix

Faure and the top army brass, citing anti-Semitism and judicial corruption in the unlawful jailing of Alfred Dreyfus, a Jewish artillery captain in the French army, for alleged espionage. Zola was convicted of libel and fled France for England to escape imprisonment. But, he was later allowed to return in time to see the government fail and Dreyfus pardoned and later exonerated. Zola said, "The truth is on the march, and nothing shall stop it." On the hundredth anniversary of Zola's article, France's Roman Catholic daily paper, *La Croix*, apologized for its anti-Semitic editorials during the Dreyfus affair.

· In February 1945, novelist, historian, and outspoken critic of the Soviet Union **Aleksandr Solzhenitsyn** was arrested for writing defamatory comments about dictator Joseph Stalin in private letters. He was officially convicted of anti-Soviet propaganda and served eight years at a labor camp before being sentenced to internal exile at Kok-Terek in northern Kazakhstan. The good news? He was awarded the 1970 Nobel Prize in Literature. The bad news? He refrained from going to Stockholm to receive his award for fear he wouldn't be allowed to reenter his home country. The next bad news? He was expelled from the Soviet Union in 1974. The next good news? He returned to Russia in 1994 after the dissolution of the Soviet Union.

THREATENED WITH DEATH (AND POSSIBLY ASSASSINATED)

· Chilean poet **Pablo Neruda** was a Nobel Prize winner. He was also a Communist, which defined much of his later writings. In the late 1940s, after he spoke out against Chilean president Gabriel González Videla, the president put out a warrant for Neruda's arrest.

Neruda fled the country with his family and didn't return from exile for five years. Nearly two decades later, the Chilean Communist Party nominated him for president, but he instead supported the Socialist Party nominee, Salvador Allende, who was elected and made Neruda ambassador to France. Then, Allende committed suicide in 1973 to avoid surrendering to right-wing troops staging a coup, and General Augusto Pinochet seized control of the country. Now, here's where the plot thickens: Neruda died suspiciously just several days later, and the cause of his death remains a mystery. In 2015, the Chilean ministry released a document stating it is possible—and even highly likely—that the Pinochet regime may have murdered Neruda!

· The "Rushdie Affair" erupted in 1988 when **Salman Rushdie**'s fourth novel, *The Satanic Verses*, was published. The novel was inspired in part by the life of the prophet Muhammad, and some Muslims felt it disparaged him. The following year, the Ayatollah Khomeini of Iran issued a *fatwa* (ruling) ordering Muslims to kill Rushdie. While Rushdie has evaded death, the controversy surrounding his novel has led to numerous killings, attempted killings, and bombings. The fatwa still remains in place as of this writing, although the Iranian government stopped officially backing it in 1998. In *The Guardian*, English writer Hanif Kureishi called the fatwa "one of the most significant events in postwar literary history."

I hope you will never face the more extreme threats described here, dear Activist, but, regardless, you're still putting yourself and your opinions out there through your art. It's a noble pursuit, and the world is a better place for it.

The Takeaway

If you're an Activist or someone with Activist tendencies, you are fired up and ready to go! Creativity is your outlet for promoting your strong opinions and influencing others in the hopes of saving—or at least changing—the world. What can you do to make the most of your creativity and idealism while also allowing a smidgen of realism to influence your actions and art?

- Get out there and change the world through art. Try to avoid feeling discouraged if people don't support the issues you care about at first; they'll come around.
- Remember, not everything you create has to have political purpose. Sheer entertainment and beauty are necessary in this world, too.
- Art with political purpose is still art first, so don't let the message get so heavy-handed it ruins the artistry or puts off the very people you want to attract.
- When you're dealing with a pressing issue, think about using promotion, social media, or direct action to give your art even greater power. Art, alone, may not always get the job done.
- Use your creativity to represent your community if you want, but don't allow yourself to be pigeonholed.
- Respond to local or global events in your own time, in your own fashion.
- Beware of the risks of doing political art, but don't let that scare you away.

Keep on fighting the good fight!

Conclusion

FOR ALL CREATIVE TYPES

〜✥〜

Creativity is intelligence having fun.

—ALBERT EINSTEIN

Now that you've ventured inside the minds and souls of luminaries representing each of the creative types, what have you discovered about your own artistic personality? Are you an A-Lister eager to occupy center stage, an Artisan trying to perfect your craft, a Game Changer seeking to do groundbreaking art, a Sensitive Soul longing to make meaning of your life and help others in the process, or an Activist determined to change the world through art? A little bit of each?

Whatever your type, learning about and continually returning to the reasons *why* creativity is so important to you will be enormously helpful—especially during those frustrating times (and we've all had them) when you can't seem to get off the mark or you're dealing with an especially intractable creative block or you're trying to reignite your creative spark.

While many traits and tendencies are associated with a particular creative type, some apply across the board, to any artist, and it's important to learn about those, too. And so, now, for something a little different, I'm going to reveal motivations and inspirations that play a role in creative people's lives *regardless* of their artistic personalities. See which ones resonate with you!

Honoring People You Love or Admire

Many artists and writers are attuned to the lives of the people who preceded them and paved a path for them—or even made their very existence possible. Maybe you're someone who wants to use your creativity to pay this debt of gratitude.

In my case, I can see my mother sitting in our 1970s-style kitchen (shiny gingham wallpaper in oranges and yellows with large flowers, brown-gold linoleum floor, a Formica table, and, yes, a landline) after dinner, catching up with her best girlfriends. She had the telephone receiver cradled under her neck, and sometimes she held a cigarette in her left hand. With her right, she doodled away on pads of paper, usually drawing geometric designs. My mother would never have considered herself an artist, and she died when I was seventeen so she never got to witness my own writing career take shape. But, please don't be fooled into thinking of her drawings as "just" doodles. I believe my mother had the urge to express herself creatively, and this was her outlet.

While my parents didn't pursue official creative paths, both of them were delighted that I wrote and painted and drew and played piano (terribly) and guitar (passably at best). When my sister and I threw them a surprise party for their twenty-fifth anniversary in the basement of our Long Island home, how did I corral them into coming downstairs, where the guests had been snuck in and were patiently waiting? By telling them I had just finished a new painting I was really excited about. They headed downstairs, nearly tripping over each other, to see it. Surprise! But I wasn't surprised—their enthusiasm reflects what so many parents who haven't had a chance to pursue creativity on a grander scale have done for their kids. And, so, honoring my parents has been very much on my mind as I've written this book. Famous creators have pursued this path, as well.

Director Steven Spielberg has made it a point to honor "The Greatest Generation," especially those who fought in World War II or survived the Holocaust.

If you've ever seen the opening sequence of Spielberg's *Saving Private Ryan*, I think you'll agree that it may be the most gripping, heart-wrenching, devastating portrayal of war in all of cinema. I, personally, wept through it the first time I saw it. It's like you're there, sloshing through the water and then storming the beaches of Normandy along with thousands of painfully young U.S. soldiers around you. Bullets are flying fast and furious, your buddy's arm has just been blown off and he goes to retrieve it, naively believing it will be sewn back on, someone to the other side of you is scream-ing in pain, the sound of gunfire is so relentless you're temporarily deafened, and you're in a hell of mud and blood and vomit with an unseen enemy, somewhere over the cliffs, spraying bullets indis-criminately down at you and everyone around you.

Spielberg made it his mission to capture the visceral experi-ence and terror of those who fought there with as much accuracy and heart as possible. As Spielberg told film critic Roger Ebert, "I wanted to bring the audience onto the stage with me and demand them to be participants with those kids who had never seen combat before in real life, and get to the top of Omaha Beach together."

As for his overriding motive in making the film? Spielberg said, "This is me being 51 years old and my dad being 81, and he fought in Burma. And my wanting to acquit his war with honor, as opposed to just using his war as the backdrop for a big action adventure picture."

Alice Walker, Pulitzer Prize–winning author of *The Color Purple*, wrote an essay, "In Search of Our Mothers' Gardens," in which she honored the black women who preceded her and who, due to slavery and ongoing oppression, had their creative gifts stifled. Or, at best, these women got to express themselves either

anonymously or through activities unrecognized as art, like garden-
ing or quilting.

And here was Walker in the 1970s, a successful African
American activist, feminist, and writer, who certainly faced her
own struggles but not the sorts of barriers blocking these women.
She describes them like this: "Our mothers and grandmothers have,
more often than not anonymously, handed on the creative spark,
the seed of the flower they themselves never hoped to see: or like a
sealed letter they could not plainly read."

Walker wanted us to know that, somehow or other, many of
them found a way to express themselves, even if their names never
appeared on their work. She also dispels the snobbish notion that
an oil painting hanging in the Metropolitan Museum of Art has
greater inherent value than, say, the magnificent flower gardens her
mother cultivated that were the talk of the neighborhood in Georgia where Walker grew up.

She recognized her mother as a true artist, writing, "I notice
that it is only when my mother is working in her flowers that she is
radiant, almost to the point of being invisible—except as Creator:
hand and eye. She is involved in work her soul must have. Ordering
the universe in the image of her personal conception of Beauty."

Think about who in your life has made it possible for you to
express yourself, creatively. Who would you want to honor, even
if indirectly, for supporting and encouraging your dreams of doing
creative work?

Allowing for the Unknown

Creativity is a mystery, one not meant to be fully solved. It's good
to embrace this mystery, knowing that the source of your creativity can be elusive, impossible to pinpoint. Isn't there something

beautiful about having this amazing force in your life that philosophy, psychology, and even science cannot fully account for? It might be the unconscious, it might be a medium who's channeling creativity through you—who knows? Whatever it is, it does its own thing and at its own pace, and you can't control it. So, just go with it.

In *Bird by Bird: Some Instructions on Writing and Life*, Anne Lamott addresses an artist's tendency to want to rush the creative process, writing, "Your unconscious can't work when you are breathing down its neck. You'll sit there going, 'Are you done in there yet, are you done in there yet?' But it is trying to tell you nicely, 'Shut up and go away.'"

This can be frustrating, especially if you're depending on your unconscious to produce magnificent work for you when your deadline is just two hours away! Giving free rein to your unconscious may also make it hard for you to explain your creative process to others who wonder what in the world you're up to when you're staring into space or putting your head down on your desk (let's hear it for power naps!).

You can take comfort from the perspective of the late, great director Mike Nichols. When he'd be working on a film, the "suits" would come around to the writers' space, wondering why they weren't *doing* anything. Nichols would put the executives in their place by explaining that, whether it looked like it or not, the writers were doing their job: *writing*.

Paul McCartney famously (and lucratively) experienced the unconscious workings of the mind, resulting in the most-recorded song in history, "Yesterday." The story goes that he woke up with a melody in his head, hurried over to the piano next to his bed, and played it, complete. In the biography *Paul McCartney: Many Years from Now*, McCartney acknowledged that he was worried he'd accidentally stolen the tune from someone else, and so he called various mates and played it for them. As he recalled, "People said to me, 'No, it's lovely, and I'm sure it's all yours.' It took me a little while to allow myself to claim it, but then like a prospector I finally staked my claim; stuck a little sign on it and said, 'Okay, it's mine!'" Amusingly, McCartney had the tune but not yet the lyrics, and so he used "scrambled eggs" as a placeholder until he came up with the infinitely better three-syllable "yesterday."

Singer-songwriter James Taylor feels he cannot claim full credit for songs arising from within him with seemingly no active participation by Taylor himself. I love how he phrases it in *Troubadours* on PBS: "Rather than writing the songs, I was just the first person to hear them."

One of the best-known stories illustrating the enigma of creativity is this: One day while J. K. Rowling was waiting and waiting for a late-running train, the *Harry Potter* characters and plotlines sprang nearly fully formed into her mind. Describing this moment in her Harvard University commencement speech, she said, "I had been writing almost continuously since the age of six but I had never been so excited about an idea before. To my immense frustration, I didn't have a functioning pen with me, and I was too shy to ask anybody if I could borrow one. I think, now, that this was probably a good thing, because I simply sat and thought, for four (delayed train) hours, and all the details bubbled up in my brain, and this scrawny, black-haired, bespectacled boy who didn't know he was a wizard became more and more real to me."

In my personal experience, when I write a newspaper or online magazine column, one of my greatest satisfactions is waking up in a panic the morning I'm planning to file it to find it's nearly fully formed in my mind and just needs to be transcribed, in a sense. Thanks, unconscious! I bet you've had experiences like this, too, in which your only role is to graciously accept the words or melody or vision as you would any gift because that's what it is—a gift.

Creativity Booster
Capturing Your Ideas First Thing in the A.M.

This is a really simple exercise with enormous benefits. The moment you open your eyes in the morning, reach for your smartphone—but *not* to check emails or social media sites. Or, go old school and keep a journal next to your bed. Write, type, or dictate thoughts relating to a creative project you're working on or an idea for a new one. Don't make the same mistake I have of thinking you'll remember that terribly clever opening line for your short story or your concept for a visual album until later in the day. It could disappear—forever—the moment you place your feet on the floor and start moving toward the rest of your day. So, take those extra few moments and capture the creative offspring of your dreams.

In a related vein, some artists and writers believe not only in the potential of the unconscious but also in the value of meditation in opening the mind to creative ideas. Filmmaker David Lynch, who has been a twice-daily practitioner and supporter of Transcendental Meditation since the early 1970s, has said it's given him access to pure consciousness. In his book *Catching the Big Fish: Meditation, Consciousness, and Creativity*, he describes the process as diving within an endless sea where ideas, instead of fish, can be caught.

Writer Mary Karr also praises the benefits of meditation, and in *The Art of Memoir* she offers this advice to aspiring writers: "Just apply your ass to chair (as someone wise once said, a writer's

only requirement) and for fifteen or twenty minutes, practice getting your attention out of your head, down to some wider expanse
in your chest or solar plexus—a place less self-conscious or skittered
or scared. The idea is to unclench your mind's claws."

Are You Genius Material?

One of the timeless questions in any genre of creativity is this: is a
genius born or made? The answer, as you'll see, has evolved over the
centuries, often saying more about society's view of human potential than it does about any definition that is set in stone.

Author Elizabeth Gilbert, in her wonderful TED talk, "Your
Elusive Creative Genius," recalls how the ancient Greeks and Ro-
mans believed spiritual beings are "assigned" to particular artists
to help them achieve greater heights than they otherwise would. In
other words, a person's innate gifts may be given an assist by an outside, invisible creature Gilbert humorously likens to Dobby, the house
elf, from the *Harry Potter* series. Then, centuries later, the Renaissance placed the artist front and center and heralded the belief that
a Michelangelo or a Leonardo *was* a genius rather than *had* a genius.
(And, thus, the A-Lister's belief in their own chosen-ness was born.)

Gilbert points to the dangers inherent in labeling someone a
genius—or, worse, in a mere mortal believing the label applies to
him or her. She attributes the early deaths, frequently due to drugs,
alcohol, or even suicide, of many of the twentieth century's greatest
artists to this perception of genius and the impossibility of living up
to it. I, personally, have never once been mistaken for a genius. But,
I imagine that after the enormous ego pleasure of being recognized
as uniquely talented or brilliant, the pressure to have to keep proving oneself worthy of the title would end up being exhausting and
ego-deflating. That's the last thing any creator needs.

Over the centuries, some of the artists considered geniuses balked at people's assumption that they coasted on their natural talent. Instead, they wanted everyone to know they possessed the Artisan-type ethos of practice-makes-perfect.

Michelangelo, the Renaissance artist who painted the ceiling of the Sistine Chapel and sculpted the iconic statue of David, didn't fully buy into the genius hype surrounding him, insisting, "If people knew how hard I worked to get my mastery, it wouldn't seem so wonderful at all."

And three centuries later, Mozart was similarly upset that people might think his talent as a composer was simply bestowed upon him. Mozart once wrote to his father, "People make a great mistake who think that my art has come easily to me. Nobody has devoted so much time and thought to composition as I."

David Shenk, author of *The Genius in All of Us*, observes that even a so-called child prodigy improves over time. Sure, Mozart wrote seven piano concertos between the ages of eleven and sixteen (doesn't everyone?). Yet, his first composition to achieve stature, "Symphony No. 29," was written ten years after his first, and it took him a couple of decades to reach his full potential with his final three symphonies, written at age thirty-two.

Our current understanding of genius reflects what Michelangelo and Mozart already believed: someone can be born with certain incomparable natural talents, but they're going to need education and encouragement and loads and loads of practice before they can ever hope to reach "genius" status.

Creative Companionship

As explored in Chapter 4, "The Sensitive Soul," doing creative projects can help alleviate feelings of loneliness if you find yourself going through periods of too much alone time. Ironically, creativity can also bring on isolation.

So much of the creative process is solitary. If you're pecking away at a keyboard or doing architectural drawings for hours on end with the occasional glimpse at Facebook or Twitter for virtual companionship, it can get pretty lonesome. And, if you're someone who tends toward melancholy or is dealing with painful memories that could bring even the most Pollyannaish person down, this goes double for you. So, how about finding methods to integrate more social interaction into your process?

Sometimes artistic pursuits can provide an "excuse" to interact with others. Artistic collaboration (covered in more detail in Chapter 2, "The Artisan") is an effective loneliness-battling strategy for many creators. It not only provides you with companionship but also might save you when you've become so close to the painful subject of your work that you begin losing perspective. Musician Sufjan Stevens had this experience.

In Chapter 4, "The Sensitive Soul," I discussed how Stevens came to terms with the loss of his mother by making the album *Carrie and Lowell.* Previously, he had released nine albums and had usually produced them himself, but he had made thirty demos of the material about his mom and stepdad and was at a loss about what to do with them. Enter Thomas Bartlett, a musician-producer friend who'd recently lost a brother to cancer. Stevens's choice to bring in a collaborator who could help him take those demos and shape them into a coherent album made all the difference between a work in progress—or possibly an abandoned project—and a completed album.

Getting out of your own head space can be really important to the creative process, not to mention your emotional well-being. You could join or attend writers' workshops, critique groups, conferences, retreats, and classes. There's also a method I call "parallel play." Picture what happens when you place two toddlers next to each other to play with trucks or assemble jigsaw puzzles. They'll each do their own thing, barely glancing at the other yet content to sit together—at least until one of them (undoubtedly a future A-Lister) gets jealous and tries to snatch a puzzle piece from the other kid. That's parallel play. For creative people, there's the grown-up version of this.

Singer-songwriter Patti Smith writes of her experience with parallel play with her friend, lover, and co-muse Robert Mapplethorpe in her memoir *Just Kids*. They ultimately pursued different artistic routes: Smith would bring rock 'n' roll's rebel spirit to poetry, and Mapplethorpe would shock the art world with his homoerotic photographs. In their early days living together in the smallest room at the famed artists' haunt, the Chelsea Hotel in New York, they just made art. As Smith described a typical night, "We gathered our colored pencils and sheets of paper and drew like wild, feral children into the night, until, exhausted, we fell into bed."

In the case of the painter Vincent van Gogh, he was a loner—not by choice—who longed for companionship beyond that of his brother, Theo, especially since Theo did not live nearby. Van Gogh, too, tried parallel play by inviting one of his few friends, painter Paul Gauguin, to his home in the town of Arles in the South of France. They painted, separately yet together, in one space. However, Van Gogh's personality issues soon drove Gauguin away, which left Van Gogh feeling abandoned and desperate. In fact, the infamous ear-cutting incident followed soon after.

Van Gogh devised another, more successful strategy (for him) for making sure he was with another person as he painted: he would do portraits of people in town and at other locales not only because he enjoyed portrait painting but also for the sake of escaping his interminable isolation. While some people were too afraid of him to pose, others did, including a shepherd in Provence; the poet Eugen

Boch, a fellow patient at the insane asylum; Monsieur Trabuc, the head attendant there; and Joseph Roulin, a postal carrier. Steven Naifeh, coauthor of *Van Gogh: The Life*, believes portraits were Van Gogh's favorite subject, describing the choice as "less artistic than it was emotional."

As for poet Donald Hall, he wasn't looking to strengthen connections with people who were alive—he was attempting to reach someone he loved who'd died. When Hall's wife, poet Jane Kenyon, was diagnosed with leukemia and died fifteen months later, he was devastated and angry. Hall had good reason to expect his wife to outlive him since he was nineteen years older and had already battled cancer twice. Instead, he lost not just his partner in love and life but also the woman who might be described as his co-muse. Or, did he?

If, as author André Maurois wrote, "A happy marriage is a long conversation which always seems too short," Hall needed to find a way to keep the conversation—and, in a sense, his marriage—going. He said in an interview with *Studio 360*, "Writing poems served me by bringing me closer to her in the moments of working on them and working them over.... And I also did it to look to her for help.... I constantly thought, 'What would Jane say here?' So there was a companionship in writing them as well.... I did, like many widowers and widows, talk to gravestones, talk to photographs on the walls, but I also sat down and—using the art that I've been trying to practice for fifty years—addressed her with my art."

In the course of reading these pages, you've gotten to identify your creative type, discover additional traits and tendencies of yours, and learn about the drives shared by all artistic personalities.

Isn't it amazing—and encouraging—to realize that the artists you adore and idolize share the very same traits, tendencies, and

Creativity Booster
Finding a Creative Companion

You might be drawn to forms of creativity that result in a lot of alone time—maybe too much. If you're finding such solitude oppressive, take a second look at the Creative Companionship section and try some of the strategies these famous artists employed. Who might serve as a collaborator? Who might engage in parallel play with you? Is there someone you'd like to address your work to and have an ongoing "conversation" with? Choose one or two approaches, and see if they make sense for you.

even fears as you do? And now, maybe for the first time, you'll have as clear a notion as these creative legends do as to *why* making art is so vitally important to you.

I hope *What's Your Creative Type?* becomes a valued companion, a cheerleader, and a coach for you in your artistic pursuits. It will be there for you when you pick up a paintbrush, type "Chapter 1" for the first time, enter various stages of a project, or pursue new directions. And it will be a resource for you as you grow and change and different aspects of your artistic personality emerge.

Whether you're an A-Lister, an Artisan, a Game Changer, a Sensitive Soul, or an Activist, I have just two more words to share with you: GO CREATE!

ACKNOWLEDGMENTS

My heartfelt thanks go out to my agent extraordinaire and former student, Amanda Annis, and the team at Trident Media; my super-sharp and super-kind editor, Stephanie Knapp, and the team at Seal Press, most especially Michael Clark, Lissa Warren, Raquel Hitt, Kevin Hanover, and Matt Weston; Kara Davison, for a book cover design I love; Blackstone Audio; awesome interns Haley Sherif, Kate Andres, and Sarah Malley; Grub Street's Muse & the Marketplace, where the initial pages of my manuscript were first read by the editor Jill Schwartzman; Emerson College, for launching me into the two careers I love, writing and teaching, giving me the freedom to design my creativity course, and workshopping my book proposal in David Emblidge's graduate publishing course; my uber-talented, enthusiastic, funny, and inspiring students at Emerson College and Boston University; Cathy Heenan, for helping me figure out my creative *why*; my warm, wonderful, witty friends, who've cheered me on; co-first-time author-friends Delia Cabe and Gina Vild—going through this experience at the same time has made it triply sweet; Stuart Schwartz, for translating legalese; my parents and sister, Taryn, and family-in-law for all their love and support; Betty Ferm and Ruby Horansky, my author idols; my son, Daniel, for always making me proud and, just as importantly, for having the same sense of humor as I do; and my husband, Matt, who makes all things seem possible.

NOTES

Introduction

ix **"To create a work of art is to create the world"**: Wassily Kandinsky, *Concerning the Spiritual in Art* (New York: Dover Publications, rev. ed., 1977).

x **"Whitman was a non-poet"**: Robert McCrum, "You're Never Too Old to Start Writing," *The Guardian*, June 26, 2010.

x **Or that Frank Sinatra prematurely retired**: Anthony Summers and Robbyn Swann, *Sinatra: The Life* (New York: Knopf, 2005).

Chapter 1: The A-Lister

1 **"The only people who are remembered"**: Eric Bogosian, *The Perforated Heart* (New York: Simon & Schuster, 2009).

7 **Consider actress Susan Sarandon's**: Helena de Bertodano, "'I'm Still a Hippie Chick': Susan Sarandon Interview," *The Telegraph*, October 4, 2010.

8 **actress Glenn Close described the relationship**: William Wolf, "It's Time for Glenn Close," *New York*, August 2, 1982.

8 **During an interview with LuPone**: Susan Stamberg, "Patti LuPone: Memoir of a Broadway Diva," *Morning Edition*, NPR, September 14, 2010.

8 **In the documentary**: *Elaine Stritch: Shoot Me*, directed by Chiemi Karasawa, Sundance Selects, 2013.

8 **And comedian Dave Chappelle**: Dave Chappelle, interviewed by James Lipton, *Inside the Actors Studio*, Bravo, February 12, 2006.

9 **Didion writes, "In many ways"**: Joan Didion, "Why I Write," *The New York Times Magazine*, December 5, 1976.

9 **She continues, "You can disguise":** Ibid.

10 **In an interview in the *Paris Review*:** Linda Kuehl, "Joan Didion: The Art of Fiction No. 71," *Paris Review* (Fall–Winter 1978).

10 **"The writer is always tricking":** Ibid.

10 **In the play *Red*:** John Logan, *Red*, Dramatists Play Service, April 27, 2010.

12 **Queen of Soul:** Aretha Franklin, quoted in "Aretha Franklin Biography," *Biography*, available at http://www.biography.com/people /aretha-franklin-9301157.

12 **Photographer Robert Mapplethorpe, in describing:** Robert Mapplethorpe, quoted in Patricia Morrisroe, *Mapplethorpe: A Biography* (New York: Random House, 2016).

12 **And here's my favorite example:** Patti LuPone, "Patti LuPone Talks Theater, Pepper Blood and Her New Play at Lincoln Center," *Time Out*, June 8, 2015.

13 **I like what he had to say about vanity:** Bertrand Russell, "Nobel Lecture: What Desires are Politically Important?" Nobel Prize Organizations, Stockholm, December 11, 1950.

13 **He defines "sheer egoism" as:** George Orwell, "Why I Write," in *Why I Write* (New York: Penguin, 2005).

14 **Orwell also believed that:** Ibid.

15 **"His early self-portrait prints":** James Hall, *The Self-Portrait: A Cultural History* (New York: Thames & Hudson, 2014).

17 **Singer Bob Marley claimed:** Quoted in "34 Years Later, Bob Marley Is About to Make History One More Time," Tom Barnes, Music.Mic, December 22, 2014, available at https://mic.com/articles/107026/bob -marley-is-about-to-become-the-defining-artist-of-2015#.hoIVuN2Fe.

17 **Author Jorge Luis Borges said:** Alastair Reid, "Neruda and Borges," *The New Yorker*, June 24, 1996.

17 **Writer James Salter said:** Nick Paumgarten, "Postscript: James Salter, 1925–2015," *The New Yorker*, June 21, 2015.

17 **And poet and novelist Sylvia Plath:** Sylvia Plath, *Unabridged Journals of Sylvia Plath* (New York: Anchor, 2000).

18 **In the book:** George Martin, quoted in Mark Hertsgaard, *A Day in the Life: The Music and Artistry of the Beatles* (New York: Delacorte Press, 1995).

18 **In the early years of Beatlemania:** John Lennon quoted in ibid.

19 **When Brian Wilson, the "mad genius":** Liam Gowing, "Brian Wilson," *A.V. Club,* August 30, 2006, available at http://www.av club.com/article/brian-wilson-14013.

19 **In response, Robbo slapped him:** Robbo, interviewed in *Banksy vs. Robbo Graffiti Wars,* directed by Jane Preston, October 2010, available at https://www.youtube.com/watch?v=WzFwO_bbnIo.

22 **Dancer/choreographer Twyla Tharp:** Twyla Tharp, *The Creative Habit: Learn It and Use It for Life* (New York: Simon & Schuster, 2006).

24 **Strayed called it, "up too high and down too low":** Cheryl Strayed, "Dear Sugar, *The Rumpus* Advice Online Column #48: Write Like a Motherfucker," *The Rumpus,* August 19, 2010. Available at http://therumpus.net/2010/08/dear-sugar-the-rumpus-advice -column-48-write-like-a-motherfucker/.

24 **"I had to write my book":** Ibid.

25 **"Write like a motherfucker":** Ibid.

25 **Famed director Alfred Hitchcock once said:** Alfred Hitchcock, quoted in Leslie H. Abramson, *Hitchcock & the Anxiety of Author-ship* (New York: Palgrave Macmillan, 2015).

25 **she muses aloud about her protagonist:** *The Hours,* directed by Stephen Daldry, Paramount Pictures and Miramax Films, 2002.

26 **When Vanessa asks what's on her mind:** Ibid.

26 **She said in a *Paris Review* interview:** "Fran Lebowitz, A Humor-ist at Work," *Paris Review* (Summer 1993).

26 **In Martin Scorsese's documentary:** *Public Speaking,* directed by Martin Scorsese, HBO, 2010.

27 **After she grows up:** Ian McEwan, *Atonement* (London: Jonathan Cape, 2001).

28 **As he told the famous photographer:** Brassaï, *Conversations with Picasso* (Chicago: University of Chicago Press, 1999).

28 **But Picasso also believed:** Ibid.

28 **As for painter and pal:** Paul Johnson, *Creators: From Chaucer and Durer to Picasso and Disney* (New York: HarperPerennial, 2007).

29 **Picasso divided women into:** Françoise Gilot and Carlton Lake, *Life with Picasso* (New York: McGraw-Hill, 1964).

29 **Picasso told her:** Ibid.

29 **He was eighty-two:** "Prostituting Picasso," *The Guardian*, March 19, 1999.

29 **And here's the coup de grace:** Ibid.

30 **Krasner once recalled:** Lee Krasner quoted in Jonathan Weinberg, *Ambition and Love in Modern American Art* (New Haven: Yale University Press, 2001).

30 **His ascendancy was announced:** Staff, "Jackson Pollock: Is He the Greatest Living Painter in the United States?" *Life*, August 8, 1949.

31 **Gaga dismissed the comparison:** Lady Gaga, interviewed by Howard Stern, *Howard Stern Show*, SiriusXM, November 12, 2013.

32 **As Heidi Klum cautions:** Heidi Klum, *Project Runway*, Bravo, December 1, 2004.

32 **Lebowitz noted that:** Fran Lebowitz, interviewed by Toni Morrison, *Public Speaking*, directed by Martin Scorsese, HBO, 2010.

33 **He tells his daughter:** *Birdman or (The Unexpected Virtue of Ignorance)*, directed by Alejandro G. Iñárritu, Fox Searchlight Pictures, 2014.

33 **With her eyes bugging out:** Ibid.

35 **She said, "Most artists create":** Lucinda Williams, interviewed by David Greene, *Morning Edition*, WBUR, February 9, 2016.

35 **Williams attributed her unflagging creativity:** Ibid.

35 **He said, "Right up to the day they died":** Geraldine Fabrikant, "Talking Money with Tony Bennett: His Heart's in San Francisco, His Money's in His Son's Hands," *The New York Times*, May 2, 1999.

36 **As she told *The Washington Post*:** Laura Hambleton, "Now 75, Jane Fonda Looks Back—and Ahead," *The Washington Post*, January 7, 2013.

36 **And she asks herself, "How can I remain":** Ibid.

36 **Streep emphasized the importance:** Karina Longworth, "Meryl Streep: Anatomy of an Actor: How the Most Respected Actress in Hollywood Learned to Stop Worrying and Love Being Laughed At," *Vanity Fair*, January 15, 2014.

38 **In response to the cruel remarks:** Carrie Fisher, "Youth is temporary, diva is forever," Twitter, December 29, 2015, 2:26 a.m.

Chapter 2: The Artisan

39 **"I know nothing in the world"**: Emily Dickinson, available at http://www.goodreads.com/quotes/82436-i-know-nothing-in-the-world-that-has-as-much.

44 **this is how he describes his discovery**: The Edge, interviewed in *It Might Get Loud*, directed by Davis Guggenheim, Sony Pictures Classics, 2008.

44 **"Just as a comedian"**: "The Edge Interview: Memory Man," *Guitar World*, November 10, 2008.

44 **"Films don't begin only when"**: "The Method Madness of Daniel Day-Lewis," *The Telegraph*, January 23, 2013.

45 **Malcolm Gladwell, in his book *Outliers*, popularized**: Malcolm Gladwell, *Outliers: The Story of Success* (New York: Little, Brown, and Company, 2008).

45 **As music historian Philip Norman**: *Shout! The Beatles in Their Generation* (New York: Simon & Schuster, 2005).

46 **It was, to paraphrase the line from the movie *Casablanca***: *Casablanca*, directed by Michael Curtiz, Warner Bros., 1942.

46 **"I thought I was the only guy"**: *Keith Richards: Under the Influence*, directed by Morgan Neville, Tremolo Productions, 2015.

47 **Yet Richards claims the stage**: Ibid.

48 **This remained true**: Winston Churchill, quoted in Amanda Vickery, "Jane Austen Through the Ages," *HistoryToday*, January 1, 2012.

49 **Dickinson's poems did not always garner positive reviews**: Thomas Bailey Aldrich, "In Re Emily Dickinson's Poems," *The Atlantic Monthly* 69, January 1892.

51 **As described by the writer**: Alex Kotlowitz, "The Best Street Photographer You've Never Heard Of," *Mother Jones* (May–June 2011).

51 **In the documentary, accomplished photographer**: Joel Meyerowitz, interviewed in *Finding Vivian Maier*, directed by John Maloof and Charlie Siskel, IFC Films, 2013.

51 **"She made {the photographs}"**: Kotlowitz, "The Best Street Photographer."

52 **Writer Truman Capote said, "To me, the greatest pleasure"**: "Truman Capote: Quotes from the Author of *Breakfast at Tiffany's*," *The Telegraph*, June 13, 2016.

52 **Painter Claude Monet declared, "Colour is":** "Monet Quotes," C. Monet Gallery, available at http://www.cmonetgallery.com/quotes .aspx.

52 **And composer Ludwig van Beethoven said, "Tones sound":** Alexander Wheelock Thayer, *The Life of Ludwig van Beethoven* (New York: Beethoven Association, 1921).

52 **Psychologist Mihaly Csikszentmihalyi calls:** Mihaly Csikszentmihalyi, *Flow: The Psychology of Optimal Experience* (New York: HarperPerennial Modern Classics, 2008).

52 **Csikszentmihalyi has pinpointed the precise moment:** Ibid.

53 **Daniel Goleman puts it this way:** Daniel Goleman, "Pondering the Riddle of Creativity," *The New York Times*, March 22, 1992.

53 **Fortunately, after some time had passed:** Stephen King, *On Writing: 10th Anniversary Edition: A Memoir of the Craft* (New York: Scribner's, 2010).

54 **As he describes it:** Ernest Hemingway, *A Moveable Feast* (New York: Scribner's, 1964).

54 **In Chapter 1, "The A-Lister":** Twyla Tharp, *The Creative Habit: Learn It and Use It for Life* (New York: Simon & Schuster, 2006).

55 **Csikszentmihalyi found that a disregard:** Daniel Goleman, "Pondering the Riddle of Creativity," *The New York Times*, March 22, 1992.

57 **Close advises young artists:** "Chuck Close's Advice to His Younger Self," *CBS This Morning*, CBS News, April 10, 2012.

57 **One of my favorite things anyone has ever said:** Ibid.

57 **"Inspiration and work ethic":** *The White Stripes: Under Great White Northern Lights*, directed by Emmett Malloy, Third Man Films, 2009.

58 **As she says, "Don't be daunted":** Elizabeth Gilbert, "Your Elusive Creative Genius," TED, Long Beach, CA, February 2009.

58 **As Isabel Allende writes:** "Isabel Allende," in *Why We Write: 20 Acclaimed Authors on How and Why They Do What They Do*, edited by Meredith Maran (New York: Plume, 2013).

58 **Anne Lamott, the author of one of my favorite books:** Anne Lamott, *Bird by Bird: Some Instructions on Writing and Life* (New York: Anchor, 1995).

58 **And more than a century earlier:** Pyotr Ilyich Tchaikovsky, quoted in Modeste Tchaikovsky, *The Life and Letters of Pyotr Ilyich Tchaikovsky*, translated by Rosa Newmarch (Honolulu: University Press of the Pacific, 2004).

60 **As novelist Jeanette Winterson writes:** Jeanette Winterson, *Art Objects: Essays on Ecstasy and Effrontery* (London: Vintage, 1997).

60 **As a teenager, she would type:** "Joan Didion: The Art of Fiction No. 71," *Paris Review* (Fall–Winter 1978).

61 **Didion described James's writing:** Ibid.

61 **As Bryson recalled:** Bill Bryson, interviewed by Ben Yagoda, *The Sound on the Page: Great Writers Talk About Style and Voice in Writing* (New York: HarperPerennial, 2005).

61 **He said, "Endlessly fussing":** Ibid.

62 **he thought of Cézanne as:** Henri Matisse and Jack D. Flam, *Matisse on Art* (New York: Phaidon, 1973).

62 **"Too bad for those without the strength":** Ibid.

62 **In *Red*, Rothko says:** *Red*, directed by John Logan, Dramatists Play Service, April 27, 2010.

63 **To White, "it meant everything":** Jack White, interviewed in *It Might Get Loud*, directed by Davis Guggenheim, Sony Pictures Classics, 2008.

64 **"It is the world's most exciting dance partnership":** Sir Frederick Ashton, quoted in David Wigg, "Were Margot Fonteyn and Rudolph [*sic*] Nureyev Secret Lovers?" *The Daily Mail*, November 26, 2009.

65 **In his passionate fashion:** Rudolf Nureyev, quoted in "Rudolf Nureyev and Margot Fonteyn: The Perfect Partnership," available at http://www.nureyev.org/rudolf-nureyev-biography-margot-fonteyn/.

65 **He also said, "We danced with one body":** Rudolf Nureyev, quoted in David Wigg, "Were Margot Fonteyn and Rudolph [*sic*] Nureyev Secret Lovers?" *The Daily Mail*, November 26, 2009.

66 **This is how BET described the duo:** "50 Greatest MC/Producer Duos: The Best MC/Producer Tag Teams of All Time," available at www.bet.com.

66 **The poet William Blake, for one:** William Blake, quoted in *William Blake*, edited by Harold Bloom, *Bloom's Classic Critical Views* series (New York: Chelsea House, 2008).

68 **The quintessential "starving artist":** Vincent Van Gogh, *My Life and Love Are One: Quotations from the Letters of Vincent Van Gogh to His Brother Theo*, edited by Irving and Jean Stone (Boulder, CO: Blue Mountain Arts, 1976).

69 **She writes, "Art does not need":** Sara Benincasa, *Real Artists Have Day Jobs (and Other Awesome Things They Don't Teach You in School)* (New York: William Morrow, 2016).

69 **Benincasa also writes, "Real artists":** Ibid.

69 **Sedaris answered, "I like to think that":** David Sedaris, interviewed by Terry Gross, *Fresh Air*, NPR, April 24, 2013.

70 **As the biographer:** Matthew J. Bruccoli, *Fitzgerald and Hemingway: A Dangerous Friendship* (New York: Carroll & Graf, 1994).

70 **But, when it comes to Artisans:** Spencer H. Harrison and David T. Wagner, "Spilling Outside the Box: The Effects of Individuals' Creative Behaviors at Work on Time Spent with Their Spouses at Home," *Academy of Management Journal*, available at http://amj.aom.org/content/59/3/841.abstract.

72 **Coppola gently admonished the students:** Francis Ford Coppola, interviewed by James Lipton, *Inside the Actors Studio*, Bravo, May 6, 2001.

72 **Eleanor quotes singer Tom Waits:** Tom Waits, quoted in Eleanor Coppola, *Notes on a Life: A Portrait of a Marriage* (New York: Nan A. Talese, 2008).

72 **In an interview with CNN, she says:** Mairi Mackay, "Coppola's Wife: 'Apocalypse Now' Was 'Out of Control,'" CNN, July 23, 2009, available at http://www.cnn.com/2009/SHOWBIZ/Movies/07/21/eleanor.coppola.apocalypse.now/index.html?iref=mpstoryview.

Chapter 3: The Game Changer

75 **"Do not go where the path may lead":** Ralph Waldo Emerson, *On Self-Reliance: Advice, Wit, and Wisdom from the Father of Transcendentalism* (New York: Skyhorse Publishing, 2014).

78 **George Bernard Shaw captured:** George Bernard Shaw, *Back to Methuselah* (Charleston, SC: BiblioBazar, 2007).

79 **In some cases, they—and possibly you:** Carl Jung, "On Psychological and Visionary Art: Notes from C. G. Jung's Lecture on Gérard de Nerval's *Aurélia*" (Princeton: Princeton University Press, 2015).

80 **visionary artists, whom I'm calling Game Changers:** John Lobell, *Visionary Creativity: How New Worlds Are Born* (New York: JXJ Productions, 2015).

81 **In one passage he says, "Throughout the centuries":** Ayn Rand, *The Fountainhead* (Indianapolis: Bobbs-Merrill Company, 1943).

81 **This, too, is a sentiment Roark espouses:** Ibid.

82 **In the film of the event:** *Marina Abramović: The Artist Is Present*, directed by Matthew Akers and Jeffrey Dupre, Show of Force Productions, 2012.

84 **Years later she confided in a friend:** Hadley Hemingway, quoted in Gioia Diliberto, "More to Hemingway's First Wife, Hadley, Than 'A Moveable Feast,'" *Chicago Tribune*, July 12, 2009.

84 **Hemingway describes his technique:** Ernest Hemingway, *A Moveable Feast* (New York: Charles Scribner's Sons, 1964).

85 **His advice to himself and aspiring authors:** Ibid.

85 **As Kaufman writes, "Expertise acquisition":** Scott Barry Kaufman, "Creativity Is Much More Than 10,000 Hours of Deliberate Practice," *Scientific American*, April 17, 2016.

85 **He further says that:** Ibid.

86 **he's quoted as saying:** George Martin, quoted in Mark Hertsgaard, *A Day in the Life: The Music and Artistry of the Beatles* (New York: Delacorte Press, 1995).

87 **It starts off with these three declarations:** Filippo Tommaso Marinetti, "Futurism Manifesto," *Le Figaro*, 1909.

87 **The founding manifesto includes:** Tristan Tzara, "Dadaism Manifesto," available at http://www.391.org/manifestos/1918-dada-manifesto-tristan-tzara.html#.V-R17Vdluvs.

88 **Here are some of their key points:** Billy Childish and Charles Thomson, "Stuckists' Manifesto," available at http://www.stuckism.com/stuckistmanifesto.html.

88 **This is how he explained the term:** Rollo May, *The Courage to Create* (New York: W. W. Norton, 1972).

89 **According to the writer Marcel Proust:** Rolf Laessøe, "Édouard Manet's 'Le Déjeuner sur L'Herbe' as a Veiled Allegory of Painting," *Artibus et Historiae* 26, no. 51 (2005).

90 **Wright was also a critic:** "Frank Lloyd Wright Dies; Famed Architect Was 89," *The New York Times*, April 10, 1959.

90 **His inventive style caused a hubbub:** Edward Lifson, "The Guggenheim at 50: A Legacy Spirals on Fifth," *All Things Considered*, NPR, August 5, 2009.

93 **Harry Allen, from *The Village Voice*:** Harry Allen, interviewed by Elizabeth Blair, "'Rapper's Delight': The One-Take Hit," *Morning Edition*, NPR, December 29, 2009.

94 **In her memoir:** Patti Smith, *Just Kids* (New York: HarperCollins, 2010).

94 **There, she reiterated:** Patti Smith, "Two Writers and a Rock Star on Stage," *The New Yorker Radio Hour*, available at http://www.newyorker.com/podcast/the-new-yorker-radio-hour/episode-6-two-writers-and-a-rock-star-on-stage.

94 **As evidence of writer Sylvia Plath's:** Sylvia Plath, *Unabridged Journals of Sylvia Plath* (New York: Anchor, 2000).

94 **"I must be a word-artist":** Ibid.

95–96 **In describing this phenomenon:** Brian Eno, "Luminous Festival," Sydney, Australia, May 28, 2009.

96 **Instead, he realized that now and then:** Ibid.

96 **In his book:** Eric Weiner, *The Geography of Genius: Lessons from the World's Most Creative Places* (New York: Simon & Schuster, 2016).

96 **As Weiner said in an interview:** "Hotbeds of Genius and Innovation Depend on These Key Ingredients," *Newshour*, PBS, July 21, 2016.

98 **The film *Pollock*:** *Pollock*, directed by Ed Harris, Sony Pictures Classics, 2001.

98 **He claimed he took one look:** Clement Greenberg quoted in Henry Adams, "Decoding Jackson Pollock," *Smithsonian Magazine* (November 2009).

101 **He called the choice "altogether literary":** Truman Capote, interviewed by George Plimpton, "The Story Behind a Nonfiction Novel," *The New York Times*, January 16, 1966.

101 **"The decision was based on a theory":** Ibid.

102 **"When I first formed my theories":** Ibid.

103 **"I fear giving short shrift":** Henri Cole, "Helen Vendler: The Art of Criticism No. 3," *Paris Review* (Winter 1996).

103 **"They will climb with you":** Jeanette Winterson, interviewed by Eleanor Wachtel, in *More Writers & Company: New Conversations*

with CBC Radio's Eleanor Wachtel (Toronto: Alfred A. Knopf Canada, 1997).

104 **"I would have to write everything":** Steve Martin, *Born Standing Up: A Comic's Life* (New York: Scribner's, 2007).

104 **Martin said to himself, "What if":** Ibid.

104 **He called Martin's approach "anti-comedy":** Rick Moranis, quoted in ibid.

105 **"To transform the word":** Norman Friedman, *E. E. Cummings: The Growth of a Writer* (Carbondale: Southern Illinois University Press, 1980).

105 **The critic George Stade:** "E. E. Cummings," Poetry Foundation, available at https://www.poetryfoundation.org/poems-and-poets /poets/detail/e-e-cummings.

107 **A little novel you might have heard of:** Alex Carter, "17 Famous Authors and Their Rejections," *Mental Floss*, March 13, 2015, available at http://mentalfloss.com/uk/books/can-you-identify-these -17-famous-authors-from-their-rejections.

107 **Writer Gertrude Stein received:** Sadie Stein, "A Rejection Is a Rejection Is a Rejection," *Paris Review*, June 27, 2013, available at http://www.theparisreview.org/blog/2013/06/27/a-rejection -is-a-rejection-is-a-rejection/.

108 **Guess who penned a rejection letter:** Alison Flood, "'It Needs More Public-Spirited Pigs': TS Eliot's Rejection of Orwell's *Animal Farm*," *The Guardian*, May 26, 2016.

108 **Building on the popularity of:** Ian Main, "BBC Comedy Script Editor Rejects *Fawlty Towers*, 1974," *The Guardian*, October 12, 2013.

108 **Superstar author Stephen King:** Alice Vincent, "The Rejection Letters: How Publishers Snubbed 11 Great Authors," *The Telegraph*, June 6, 2014.

108 **But when he was starting out, his drawings:** Jennifer M. Wood, "10 Rejection Letters Sent to Famous People," *Mental Floss*, available at http://mentalfloss.com/article/55416/10-rejection-letters-sent -famous-people.

109 **Seeking to be helpful:** Michael Schuab, "J. K. Rowling Reveals Two Rejection Letters She Got for 'The Cuckoo's Calling,'" *The LA Times*, March 29, 2016.

Chapter 4: The Sensitive Soul

111 **"Sometimes I wonder how all those"**: Graham Greene, *Ways of Escape* (New York: Simon & Schuster, 1980).

116 **"You must not fear"**: Anaïs Nin, *The Diary of Anaïs Nin*, vol. 4: 1944–1947 (New York: Mariner Books, 1972).

117 **She formulated the "need theory of self-expression"**: Alice Weaver Flaherty, *The Midnight Disease: The Drive to Write, Writer's Block, and the Creative Brain* (New York: Mariner Books, 2005).

117 **George Orwell called this urge to express oneself**: George Orwell, "Why I Write," in *Why I Write* (New York: Penguin, 2005).

118 **In *Art as Therapy*, Alain de Botton**: Alain de Botton and John Armstrong, *Art as Therapy* (London: Phaidon Press, 2013).

118 **And, as Flaherty points out**: Flaherty, *The Midnight Disease*.

118 **"I don't think sadness is always devastating"**: Adele, interviewed by Matt Lauer, *Today*, NBC, December 7, 2015.

119 **So, if you find yourself wanting for material**: William Saroyan, *The Daring Young Man on the Flying Trapeze* (New York: New Directions Publishing, 1997).

120 **The poet John Berryman, for one, even claimed**: Peter Stitt, "The Art of Poetry No. 16," *Paris Review* (Winter 1972).

120 **In his words, "The sun began to set"**: Edvard Munch, quoted in William Lee Adams, "The Dark Side of Creativity: Depression + Anxiety x Madness = Genius?" CNN, January 22, 2014.

120 **Munch believed his anxiety was essential to his creativity**: Ibid.

121 **Writer Mary Karr, who has revealed her battles**: Nina Puro, "Mary Karr: David Foster Wallace and I Kept Each Other Alive," *Salon*, May 23, 2013.

121 **The avant-garde dramatist Antonin Artaud**: Kay Redfield Jamison, *Touched with Fire: Manic-Depressive Illness and the Artistic Temperament* (New York: Simon & Schuster, 1996).

121 **While that sounds more than a little unsanitary**: Leo Tolstoy, *What Is Art?* (New York: Penguin Classics, 1996).

122 **Author Sherwood Anderson told his son**: Dorie McCullough Lawson, *Posterity: Letters of Great Americans to Their Children* (New York: Knopf Doubleday Publishing Group, 2004).

122 **Robert Lowell mused:** Robert Lowell, *Collected Poems*, edited by Frank Bidart and David Gewanter (New York: Farrar, Straus & Giroux, 2003).

123 **Poet Anne Sexton said:** Anne Sexton, available at http://www.goodreads.com/quotes/1529877-poetry-led-me-by-the-hand-out-of-madness.

123 **And author Jeanette Winterson:** Jeanette Winterson, *Art Objects: Essays on Ecstasy and Effrontery* (London: Vintage, 2013).

123 **Writer Thomas Williams:** Thomas Williams, quoted in Gina Barreca, "Inside the Writers' Conference: A Conversation Between Gina Barreca and Andre Dubus III," *Huffington Post*, June 27, 2012, available at http://www.huffingtonpost.com/gina-barreca/writers-conference-value-andre-dubus-iii_b_1631261.html.

123 **But, as de Botton reminds us, suffering, on its own:** Alain de Botton, *How Proust Can Change Your Life* (New York: Vintage, 2013).

123 **As she described it:** Yayoi Kusama, "Yayoi Kusama: When I Wanted to Commit Suicide, My Doctor Encouraged Me to Paint More," *The Telegraph*, October 23, 2013.

124 **"It was a semi-spiritual, life-saving moment":** Andre Dubus III, interviewed by Zachary Petit, "Meet the Real Andre Dubus III," *Writer's Digest*, July 31, 2012.

124 **"Writing carried me":** Augusten Burroughs, *Lust & Wonder: A Memoir* (New York: St. Martin's Press, 2016).

125 **In 2010, researchers did an analysis:** H. L. Stuckey and J. Nobel, "The Connection Between Art, Healing, and Public Health: A Review of Current Literature," *American Journal of Public Health* 100, no. 2 (2010): 254–263, available at http://doi.org/10.2105/AJPH.2008.156497.

125 **In another study:** K. J. Petrie et al., "Effect of Written Emotional Expression on Immune Function in Patients with Human Immunodeficiency Virus Infection: A Randomized Trial," *Psychosomatic Medicine* (March–April 2004), available at http://www.ncbi.nlm.nih.gov/pubmed/15039514.

125 **In 2001, the results of a study:** Gene D. Cohen, "The Creativity and Aging Study," National Endowment for the Arts, April 30,

2006, available at https://www.arts.gov/sites/default/files/CnA
-Rep4-30-06.pdf.

127 **Marcel Proust believed that "griefs":** Alain de Botton, *How Proust Can Change Your Life* (New York: Vintage, 2013).

127 **O'Rourke said in an interview:** Joyce Carol Oates, "Why We Write About Grief," *The New York Times*, February 26, 2011.

127 **In *Torch*, the daughter, Claire, acknowledges:** Cheryl Strayed, *Torch* (New York: Vintage, 2012).

127 **In her roman à clef, *Heartburn*, the heroine:** Nora Ephron, *Heartburn* (New York: Vintage, 1996).

129 **"Seems like much of my youth was spent trying":** Francis Ford Coppola, interviewed by James Lipton, *Inside the Actors Studio*, Bravo, May 6, 2001.

129 **"I just kind of cooked up a fantasy world":** Ibid.

130 **In the introduction to *The Diary of Frida Kahlo*:** Carlos Fuentes, *The Diary of Frida Kahlo: An Intimate Portrait* (New York: Abrams, 2005).

131 **As she wrote in her journal, "Anguish and pain":** Ibid.

131 **In an article about Kahlo in the *Boston Globe*:** Sebastian Smee, "Too Hot to Handle: Kahlo's Raw Intensity, Euphoric Impact," *The Boston Globe*, January 26, 2016.

132 **Blige said in an interview:** Vaziri Aidin, "Mary J. Blige Beats High Odds," *SFGate*, October 17, 2016.

133 **He captures music's unique impact:** Oliver Sacks, *Musicophilia* (New York: Vintage, 2008).

133 **Writer James Baldwin believed the only value in suffering is:** James Baldwin, "The Artist's Struggle for Integrity," New York City's Community Church, New York, Fall 1962.

133 **he responded, "Before I had":** Claire Bidwell Smith, "The Rumpus Interview with Kenny Porpora," *The Rumpus*, February 4, 2015, available at http://therumpus.net/2015/02/the-rumpus -interview-with-kenny-porpora/.

136 **In one entry:** Sylvia Plath, *Unabridged Journals of Sylvia Plath* (New York: Anchor, 2000).

136 **But, he also acknowledged how depression has fueled masterpieces:** William Styron, "Darkness Visible," *Vanity Fair* (December 1989).

137 **A 2008 study, conducted by psychiatrist Nancy Andreasen:** N. C. Andreasen, "The Relationship Between Creativity and Mood Disorders," *Dialogues in Clinical Neuroscience* 10, no. 2 (2008).

138 **"There's something about the experience":** Kay Redfield Jamison, *Touched with Fire: Manic-Depressive Illness and the Artistic Temperament* (New York: Simon and Schuster, 1996).

139 **Writer Dave Eggers, who is no stranger to suffering:** Dave Eggers, "I Was Recording Songs as a Means of Grieving," *The Guardian*, March 26, 2015.

139 **In an interview with Eggers:** Sufjan Stevens, interviewed by Dave Eggers, in ibid.

140 **Poet Robert Lowell captured the difficulty:** Kay Redfield Jamison, *Touched with Fire: Manic-Depressive Illness and the Artistic Temperament* (New York: Simon and Schuster, 1996).

140 **Joplin grew up:** Virginia Woolf, *A Room of One's Own* (London: Albatross Publishers, 2015).

140 **Joplin had "suffered the worst fate":** Ellen Willis, "Janis Joplin: A Remembrance," *Rolling Stone*, November 18, 1976.

141 **In the same documentary, her ex said of her:** *Janis: Little Girl Blue*, directed by Amy Berg, PBS, 2015.

141 **Another bandmate, Dave Getz, teared up:** Ibid.

142 **"I wrote so I could say":** Sarah Manguso, *Ongoingness: The End of a Diary* (Minneapolis: Graywolf Press, 2015).

142 **"How much space for remembering":** Elizabeth Alexander, *The Light of the World: A Memoir* (New York: Grand Central Publishing, 2015).

142 **"I write to fix him in place":** Ibid.

Chapter 5: The Activist

145 **"Poets are the unacknowledged legislators of the world":** Percy Bysshe Shelley, "A Defence of Poetry," *Essays, Letters from Abroad, Translations and Fragments* (London: Edward Moxon, 1840).

150 **He felt *compelled* to write with an activist aim:** George Orwell, "Why I Write," in *Why I Write* (New York: Penguin, 2005).

150 **Kingsolver believes creators have a duty:** Barbara Kingsolver, "Jabberwocky," *High Tide in Tucson: Essays from Now or Never* (New York: HarperCollins, 1995).

152 **One of the panelists:** Andre Dubus III, Newton Festival of the Arts, Newton Free Library, Newton, MA, May 10, 2016.

152 **"So what's a writer to do?"** Francine Prose, "Is the Writer's Only Responsibility to His Art?" *The New York Times*, January 19, 2016.

153 **When he wrote the poem:** W. H. Auden, "In Memory of W. B. Yeats," in *Another Time* (New York: Random House, 1940).

154 **And yet, when asked, Yorke insisted:** Thom Yorke, interviewed by Sarah Burton, "Truth in the Hands of Artists," *Resonance Magazine*, November 23, 2003.

154 **One of Yorke's chief criticisms:** Ibid.

154 **He believes political literature is best:** Italo Calvino, *The Uses of Literature* (New York: Houghton Mifflin Harcourt, 1986).

154 **And, in a more lyrical style:** Ibid.

154 **Alice Walker, who's been instrumental:** Alice Walker, *Anything We Love Can Be Saved: A Writer's Activism* (New York: Ballantine Books, 1998).

154 **"Now I know that":** Ibid.

155 **Take V. S. Naipaul, who, in his acceptance speech:** "Nobel Lecture: Two Worlds," Nobel Prize Organization, Stockholm, December 7, 2001.

155 **"Not long ago, a novelist could believe":** Don DeLillo, interviewed by Lorrie Moore, "Look for a Writer and Find a Terrorist," *The New York Times*, June 9, 1991.

155 **Jonathan Franzen also fretted:** Jonathan Franzen, "Why Bother?," in *How to Be Alone: Essays* (New York: Farrar, Straus & Giroux, 2002).

157 **"Art may not be a blunt instrument":** Howard Zinn, interviewed by Sarah Burton, "Truth in the Hands of Artists," *Resonance Magazine*, November 23, 2003.

157 **Zinn understood a single play:** Ibid.

159 **"Now I understand what you have to do":** John Lennon, quoted in Laurie Ulster, "The Life & Legacy of John Lennon's 'Imagine,'" *Biography*, available at http://www.biography.com/news/john-lennon-imagine-song-facts.

160 **"I used to want to save the world":** Banksy, interviewed by Lauren Collins, "Banksy Was Here," *The New Yorker*, May 14, 2007.

160 "All art is political in some way": Rachel Campbell Johnston, interviewed by Lizzie Crocker, "Why Banksy's Art Is Such a Deadly Political Weapon," The Daily Beast, January 25, 2016.

160 "He uses art as a weapon": Ibid.

161 But then, as he recalls: JR, "My Wish: Use Art to Turn the World Inside Out," TED, Long Beach, CA, March 2011.

164 "People that I love tell me I go too far sometimes": Dave Chappelle, interviewed by James Lipton, Inside the Actors Studio, Bravo, February 12, 2006.

164 she acknowledged at the Tribeca Film Festival: Amy Schumer, "Tribeca Talks: Inside Amy Schumer," Tribeca Film Festival, New York, 2015.

165 I believe the central challenge for you: George Orwell, "Why I Write," in Why I Write (New York: Penguin, 2005).

165 "I have always tried to": Rick Moody, "Why I Write," The Daily Beast, February 1, 2013.

166 I first became aware: Sarah Kay, "If I Should Have a Daughter," TED, Long Beach, CA, March 2011.

167 "If you choose to write a play": Eve Ensler, "Is Art a Call to Action, or a Distraction?" Harvard Kennedy School PolicyCast, Cambridge, MA, February 16, 2016.

169 "Once I was in the civil-rights milieu": James Baldwin, interviewed by Jordan Elgrably, "The Art of Fiction No. 78," Paris Review (Spring 1984).

170 "I'm always being put in this position": Sam Fragoso, "'We're in Disarray': An Interview with Spike Lee," The Atlantic Monthly, February 14, 2015.

170 The Asbury Park Press posted: Chris Jordan, "Bruce Springsteen and 9/11: 'We Need You Now,'" Asbury Park Press, September 11, 2016, available at http://www.app.com/story/entertainment/music/2016/09/09/bruce-springsteen-and-911-we-need-you-now/90111446/,

172 Laura Miller, book critic for Salon: Laura Miller, "Why We Haven't Seen a Great 9/11 Novel," Salon, September 10, 2011, available at http://www.salon.com/2011/09/10/9_11_and_the_novel/.

174 In 2003, during the Iraq War: Natalie Maines, quoted in "Dixie Chicks Pulled from Air After Bashing Bush," CNN, March 14, 2003,

available at http://www.cnn.com/2003/SHOWBIZ/Music/03/14
/dixie.chicks.reut/.

175 **On September 17, 2001, less than a week after the 9/11 attacks:**
Bill Maher, *Politically Incorrect*, HBO, September 17, 2001.

175 **"I can write but have lost the joy":** Oscar Wilde, quoted in Richard
Ellman, *Oscar Wilde* (New York: Knopf, 1987).

176 **In a TED film:** Ai Weiwei, interviewed in "Ai Weiwei Detained.
Here Is His TED Film," TED, available at http://blog.ted.com
/ai-weiwei-detained-here-is-his-ted-film/.

177 **"The truth is on the march":** Émile Zola, "J'accuse!..." *L'Aurore*,
January 13, 1898.

178 **English writer Hanif Kureishi:** Hanif Kureishi, "Looking Back at
Salman Rushdie's *The Satanic Verses*," *The Guardian*, September
14, 2012.

Conclusion

181 **"Creativity is intelligence having fun":** Albert Einstein, available at http://www.goodreads.com/quotes/37706-creativity-is
-intelligence-having-fun.

183 **As Spielberg told film critic:** Steven Spielberg, interviewed by
Roger Ebert, "Private Spielberg," available at http://www.rogerebert
.com/interviews/private-spielberg.

183 **Spielberg said, "This is me being 51 years old":** Ibid.

184 **"Our mothers and grandmothers":** Alice Walker, "In Search of
Our Mothers' Gardens," in *In Search of Our Mothers' Gardens:
Womanist Prose* (San Diego: Harcourt Brace Jovanovich, 1983).

184 **She recognized her mother as a true artist:** Ibid.

185 **"Your unconscious can't work when":** Anne Lamott, *Bird by Bird:
Some Instructions on Writing and Life* (New York: Anchor, 1995).

185 **As he recalled, "People said to me":** Barry Miles, *Paul McCartney:
Many Years from Now* (New York: Henry Holt, 1997).

186 **"Rather than writing the songs":** James Taylor, interviewed in
Troubadours, directed by Morgan Neville, PBS, March 2, 2011.

186 **Describing this moment:** J. K. Rowling, "The Fringe Benefits of
Failure," TED-Ed, Boston, 2008.

187 **In his book:** David Lynch, *Catching the Big Fish: Meditation, Consciousness, and Creativity* (New York: Jeremy P. Tarcher/Penguin, 2006).

187 **"Just apply your ass to chair":** Mary Karr, *The Art of Memoir* (New York: HarperCollins, 2015).

188 **Author Elizabeth Gilbert, in her wonderful TED talk:** Elizabeth Gilbert, "Your Elusive Creative Genius," TED, Long Beach, CA, February 2009.

189 **Michelangelo, the Renaissance artist:** Michelangelo, available at http://www.brainyquote.com/quotes/authors/m/michelangelo.html.

189 **Mozart once wrote to his father:** Wolfgang Amadeus Mozart, quoted in Jackson J. Spielvogel, *Western Civilization* (Belmont, CA: Wadsworth, 2000).

189 **David Shenk, author of:** David Shenk, *The Genius in All of Us: New Insights into Genetics, Talent, and IQ* (New York: Anchor, 2011).

190 **Previously, he had released nine albums:** Sufjan Stevens, interviewed by Dave Eggers, "I Was Recording Songs as a Means of Grieving," *The Guardian*, March 26, 2015.

191 **As Smith described a typical night:** Patti Smith, *Just Kids* (New York: HarperCollins, 2010).

192 **Steven Naifeh, coauthor of *Van Gogh: The Life*, believes portraits:** Steven Naifeh, interviewed by Morley Safer, "The Life and Death of Vincent Van Gogh," *60 Minutes*, CBS, 2012.

192 **"A happy marriage is":** André Maurois, available at http://www.brainyquote.com/quotes/quotes/a/andremauro108305.html.

192 **"Writing poems served me":** Donald Hall, interviewed by Kurt Anderson, "Special Guest: Donald Hall," *Studio 360*, WNYC, 2003.

ABOUT THE AUTHOR

Photo © Loren Sklar

Meta Wagner writes about creativity and pop culture, most notably as a contributor to *The Boston Globe* opinion pages and a former columnist for *PopMatters*. Her commentary and feature articles have also appeared in *Huffington Post*, *Chicago Tribune*, *Salon*, *Boston Globe Magazine*, and *Wall Street Journal Custom Studios*. She teaches at Emerson College, where she also received her MFA, and at Boston University and Grub Street, the country's leading literary arts center. Meta lives in the Boston area with her husband and son (when he stops by).